Other books in the *Walking the West* series:

Walking the East Mojave
Walking Los Angeles
Walking Southern California
Walking the California Coast
Walking California's State Parks

Walking
Santa Barbara

City Strolls &
Country Hikes

John McKinney
Cheri Rae

HarperCollins*West*

A Division of HarperCollins*Publishers*

HarperCollinsWest and the author, in association with the Rainforest Action Network, will facilitate the planting of two trees for every one tree used in the manufacture of this book.

Maps and chapter design by Chip Rowley, Art, Planning & Design
Typography by Jim Cook/Book Design & Typography
Illustrations:
Janice Blair: 18, 29, 32, 42, 49, 59, 61, 70, 78, 81, 85, 90, 139
Steve Hoegerman: 20, 45, 53, 54, 106
Reininga Corporation: Field/Paoli Architects: 51
Santa Barbara Botanic Garden: 39, 40, 144, 149, 162

This book was previously published as *Walk Santa Barbara* by Olympus Press in 1990.

FIRST HARPERCOLLINS EDITION

LIBRARY OF CONGRESS CATALOGING-IN-PUBLICATION DATA
McKinney, John, 1952–
        Walking Santa Barbara: city strolls, country hikes / John
McKinney. —1st HarperCollins ed.
            p. cm.
        Rev. ed. of: Walk Santa Barbara / Cheri Rae, 1990.
        Includes index.
        ISBN 0-06-258509-6
        1. Walking—California—Santa Barbara County—Guidebooks.
        2. Hiking—California—Santa Barbara County—Guidebooks.
        3. Santa Barbara County (Calif.)—Guidebooks. I. Rae, Cheri,
1953– Walk Santa Barbara. II. Title.
GV99.42.C22S3176   1994   93-14605
796.5'1'0979491—dc20   CIP

        94   95   96   97   98   **CWI**   10 9 8   7 6 5 4 3 2 1

This edition is printed on acid-free paper that meets the American National Standards Institute Z39.48 Standard.

Contents

Stand Fast Santa Barbara!

Romance is the greatest asset of California. It has been for more than 350 years. To all this centuried romance, Santa Barbara is legitimate and favorite heiress—about the only one left that has not yet traded away her birthright.

You hold the last of that California which has shone for centuries in song and story, which has fascinated the world and put a new sentiment and beauty in American life.

CHARLES F. LUMMIS
Santa Barbara Morning Press, 1923

Introduction

S ANTA BARBARA isn't the only place in the world with a beautiful city center, inspiring coastline or rugged backcountry. But only Santa Barbara can boast of all three of these attributes. And only in Santa Barbara can the pleasures of city and country be so easily—and enjoyably—explored on foot.

This book, then, is your invitation to explore a place like no other, an opportunity to walk through neighborhoods that beckon, through a natural world that delights. Walking Santa Barbara is a chance for visitors to get an intimate look, for busy natives a chance to slow down and smell the roses.

To walk through a city is to do much more than see it. Walking involves every sense. When you walk through Santa Barbara, you see the magnificent natural setting and beautiful architecture, and you also hear the birds and church bells, fill your lungs with fresh air, and feel the sunshine on your shoulders. You can read the unique commemorative tiles that mark historical events, you may overhear a heated political discussion at a sidewalk café, you can stop at a lovely corner flower stand and buy a token of your affection for a cherished companion.

And to walk through Santa Barbara's foothill canyons and along its coastline is to see nature intimately: Smell the sage, listen to the murmur of a little creek, experience the thousand and one pleasures of the trail. At the shore, taste the salt air, hear the cry of the gull and the bark of the sea lions, feel the sand beneath your feet.

Walking is by no means the only way to see Santa Barbara. You can rent a car, as thousands do, get one of those terrible tourist maps and get lost like everyone else. (We Santa Barbarans are always happy to give directions, to explain where you missed the turn for the Mission, the Botanic Garden or the Biltmore.) By all means, take the scenic drive, the trolley bus tour and/or the harbor cruise.

No, walking isn't the only way to see Santa Barbara; it's simply the best way. We've offered forty of our favorite walks, short and long, for your enjoyment. Even the most casual stroller will find Santa Barbara a pedestrian-friendly town and be able to navigate to the major sights with this guide. The practiced walker and avid hiker will also find in these pages many miles of pathways to follow.

A word about walking. Now that we've preached the gospel of walking, we hope you won't lose confidence in the authors if we confess just a little ambivalence about the word. The popular media image of a walker these days is one of those overheated, arm-swinging, watch-watching fitness freaks. No, the walker we have in mind is at least as interested in aesthetics as athletics.

Other words have their merit. Certainly strolling is a way to go. Sauntering conveys a certain *joie de vivre*. Even hiking is okay; this guide includes backcountry trails that will challenge the avid hiker.

Actually, the word we like best for the spirit we wish to convey, is Spanish and has no English counterpart. The word is *paseo*. A paseo can be loosely translated as a leisurely walk, an unbusinesslike excursion, a pleasurable picnic. A paseo is also a special place; you'll visit many of them in Santa Barbara.

The Spanish named not only the journey but the destinations; today, Spanish street names abound. The early Catholic padres also named peaks, valleys, rivers and canyons after their favorite saints, and Spanish words make up much of our geographical vocabulary: *cañon, rio, arroyo, punta, camino, mar.*

But Santa Barbara has embraced not only the culture of its first Spanish, and later Mexican, inhabitants, it has borrowed liberally from the entire Mediterranean. And the city has used its Mediterranean style to sell itself to the world. "See America's Riviera," invited the travel brochures. Declared an 1886 brochure: "Travelers in quest of the beautiful may no longer 'See Naples and die,' but visit Santa Barbara and live."

Santa Barbara is a Mediterranean city nestled in a picturesque setting that easily rivals any Old World locale. The word "Mediterranean" conjures up images of white buildings with tiled roofs and wrought-iron gates; stone-lined walkways and colorful plazas; alfresco dining in a convivial atmosphere; warm breezes and palm-lined beaches. It also suggests a civilized style, an appreciation for arts and culture, casual living, and warm, inviting hospitality.

But Santa Barbara is more than a Mediterranean city. It's a Mediterranean coast as well. In Santa Barbara, waves lap at broad, sandy beaches; a fleet of fishing boats bob in the harbor and palm trees sway in the cooling breeze.

On sun-drenched Santa Barbara hillsides grow drought tolerant plants, similar to those found in Mediterranean terrain. We call this Mediterranean flora chaparral. To Spanish settlers, scrub oak looked like a plant from back home that they called *chaparro*. The territory where chaparro grows we now call chaparral, and that's why cowboys wear "chaps."

Unquestionably Santa Barbara shares a sea-tempered climate—the warm days, the cool nights, the short, rainy winters—with Spain, Greece, Italy, North Africa and the South of France. The south-facing Santa Barbara coast and the Santa Ynez Mountains behind the city seem bathed in that soft, magical Mediterranean light.

Getting to know Santa Barbara means walking in both the city and country. In the city, lovely residential neighborhoods suggest leisurely strolling; shaded paseos offer unique shopping, and a few frankly tourist-y destinations simply should not be missed. But if you never stray from the sidewalk, and head into the backcountry far from the shops and parking lots, you won't really see Santa Barbara. A variety of trails head straight into the natural beauty and colorful history of the local mountains.

There's a pathway—through the city, the coast, the country—waiting to take you wherever you want to go.

Santa Barbara—A Brief History

On June 29, 1925, a severe earthquake shook Santa Barbara, damaging and destroying much of downtown. While human casualties were fortunately few, the damage to buildings was severe.

The way Santa Barbara was built—and rebuilt—after the quake was astonishing in its speed. (In 1926, the Better Homes in America jury judged Santa Barbara to be the most beautiful residential environment in the nation.)

But even more astonishing than the speed of the construction was its quality and design. After the quake, citizens and civic leaders realized they had a golden opportunity to create a unique community, a chance for Santa Barbara as one architect put it, "to make of itself the most romantic, beautiful and best-planned city in Western America."

What followed, particularly during the years 1925-30 was the full flowering of Mission Revival and Spanish Revival architecture that today makes Santa Barbara so distinctive. How that particular look was adopted, and along with it a Mediterranean lifestyle, is a story that begins more than a century-and-a-half before the big earthquake.

It's a story of the Chumash Indians, Spanish, Mexican and American and European peoples. Each group was influenced by succeeding powers; present-day Santa Barbara owes much of its richness to its past.

The first people to inhabit the Santa Barbara area were the Chumash Indians. For nearly 10,000 years, the population flourished in the mild climate, subsisting on the abundant food sources they found in the waters and on the land. They were excellent fishermen who navigated the waters of the Channel Islands in plank canoes known as

"tomolo." Although their society was preliterate, their basketry and rock drawings indicate a sophisticated knowledge of astronomy, and other artifacts suggest the Chumash were accomplished traders and architects who participated in their own religion, Chinigchinich.

The arrival of the Spanish signalled the decline, and eventual end, of Santa Barbara's native population.

In 1542, Portuguese navigator Juan Rodriguez Cabrillo, sailing for Spain, was the first European to glimpse the Santa Barbara coast. Some years later, in 1602, a priest who served the crew of Sebastian Vizcaino named the area Santa Barbara after Saint Barbara, who (he believed) heard the fervent prayers of the frightened sailors and guided the navigators through the narrow channel during a terrible storm, coincidentally on her Feast Day, December 4.

Sergeant José Francisco de Ortega, who served as a trail scout to Captain Gaspar de Portolá, was the first European to set foot in the area, in 1769. Some years later, Ortega was appointed to be the first commandante of the Santa Barbara royal fortress, a military outpost established to defend and maintain the Spanish Empire's claim to the area. On Saint Barbara's Day in 1786, the Mission was founded to reinforce the Spanish empire's religious interest as well.

Santa Barbara was affected by international relations when Mexico revolted against Spanish rule; the Treaty of Córdova transferred Spain's California holdings to Mexico in 1822.

During the short period of Mexican rule, the Mission was secularized, and much of its property was divided into ranchos, where many residents participated in the hide-and-tallow trade. Former soldiers married local women, built adobe tile-roofed houses and settled into comfortable lives.

The streets of Santa Barbara bear the names of many of the influential families of this time: de la Guerra, Carrillo, Cota and Gutierrez among them. Social festivities were colorful and frequent; in the classic *Two Years Before the Mast,* Richard Henry Dana described a three-day wedding celebration.

Most of western North America came under American control with the conclusion of the Mexican War in 1848. In quick succession, Santa Barbara was designated a county seat, incorporated as a city, and became part of the State of California, which entered the Union on September 9, 1850.

The city was surveyed in 1851 by a sea captain who possessed questionable credentials; his unfortunately sloppy work resulted in a city grid that runs curiously counter to the norm. Santa Barbara's northeast-northwest (rather than north-south) orientation has confused visitors and residents ever since.

In his 1873 travel guide, *California: For Health, Pleasure, and Residence,* Charles Nordhoff extolled the virtues of Santa Barbara's mild climate, scenic location, and.abundant natural hot springs in the nearby backcountry. His enthusiasm surely helped establish Santa Barbara as a desirable destination for "invalids," as they called them in Victorian times.

But before the city's reputation as "the Sanitarium of the Pacific"

got too firmly entrenched, boosters began building luxury residence and accommodation and marketing Santa Barbara as an upscale winter resort town for the East Coast and European wealthy. As transportation to Santa Barbara improved (the completion of Stearns Wharf passenger steamer dock, the completion of the Southern Pacific tracks and train depot), a more middle-class visitor came to holiday.

During the first two decades of the twentieth century, two industries took hold in Santa Barbara. One was the airplane factory run by the Lockheed brothers, the other was the Flying A Film Studios, which at one time had the largest and most modern production facility in the world. Alas, for Santa Barbara's future as an aerospace center and/or entertainment capital, Lockheed moved south to Burbank, the Flying A to Hollywood.

The City Today

For its size (just 18 square miles, population less than 100,000), Santa Barbara offers an surprising number of cultural attractions: First-class theatres, museums of art and natural history, a symphony orchestra, several colleges and a university, and many regularly scheduled festivals celebrating the city's unique historic and ethnic background.

But there's been trouble in paradise—plenty of it. The city has survived its share of natural disasters, including several earthquakes and devastating fires (the Painted Cave Fire of 1990 that received international attention). Periods of extended drought are a fact of life in the area, residents and visitors must carefully conserve precious water resources. And, as in most American cities, the political debates continue to rage over issues that include growth/no-growth, a permanent solution to the water shortage, a homeless population and the numerous ills that afflict the poor and unfortunate.

Still, Santa Barbara remains one of the most desirable destinations in the world. Foreign tourists literally arrive by the busload. Some fans of the long-running television soap opera "Santa Barbara" arrive hoping to find the glitzy world of the Capwell and Lockridge families. Instead, they discover a modern city that's proud of its history, a small town that offers big-city services, a caring community where neighbors still know each other and extend themselves to those in need.

And that's what living, what traveling is all about, isn't it?

Transportation

Unlike other Southern California cities, Santa Barbara offers plenty of regularly scheduled public transportation. Although it's easy to get around town on foot, when you incorporate a bus or trolley into your walking adventure, you can cover more ground in a shorter period of time. For drivers, a word of caution about parking in Santa Barbara. Downtown streets offer free 90-minute parking; the city also employs a fleet of very efficient parking police to enforce the 90-minute limit. Don't be tempted to overstay your limit! A number of city parking lots also offer free parking for 90 minutes, and charges per hour afterward.

☐ *Downtown Transit Center*
The centrally located Downtown Transit Center (at Chapala and Carrillo, just one block west of the 1000 block of State Street, is the depot for Santa Barbara's Metropolitan Transit District (MTD) system. The building provides travelers with shelter from the elements and plenty of information. Pick up a copy of MTD's *The Bus Book,* for detailed route information. The city and MTD provide a regularly scheduled downtown/waterfront shuttle service for just twenty-five cents.

Where possible, MTD route information has been provided in the "Transportation" section of the walk descriptions. Refer to the MTD map in the "Information Sources" of this guide.

☐ *Santa Barbara Trolley Company*
The Santa Barbara Trolley Company operates daily from 10 A.M. to 6 P.M. The narrated tours, aboard old-fashioned trolley cars, leave from Cabrillo Boulevard at Stearns Wharf every 90 minutes throughout the day. The trolley ride is a pleasant way to become familiar with the sights around the city.

☐ *Amtrak Station*
Located just steps away from the massive Moreton Bay Fig Tree, close to downtown, beaches and the freeway, is Santa Barbara's lovely Spanish train station. Built in 1905 in Mission Revival style, it's a graceful building that reflects the Spanish influence in Santa Barbara.

Amtrak service, both north and south, is regularly scheduled

RAILWAY STATION

through Santa Barbara. Although the service has yet to catch up with the convenience and affordability of European service, the train is a way for north- and south-bound travelers to reach Santa Barbara from San Francisco, San Luis Obispo, Ventura, Los Angeles, Fullerton, San Diego and several more towns and cities along the coast.

☐ *Greyhound Bus Station*
Located next door to the Downtown Transit Center, the Greyhound Bus Station provides frequent, low-cost departures to points north, east and south.

☐ *Santa Barbara Municipal Airport*
Major airlines operate out of the Spanish-style Santa Barbara Municipal Airport, providing non-stop service to metropolitan areas throughout the nation, along with regional and commuter flights to California destinations. The MTD offers regular bus service from the airport to town.

Santa Barbara for Walkers

Before setting out to explore Santa Barbara on foot, make sure you're equipped with the right gear: comfortable shoes, sunscreen, sunglasses and a hat, a lightweight windbreaker or jacket, and a day pack or fanny pack. Bring water and a snack. Plan your day before you head out and pack lunches or purchase them en route to your destination. There are many tempting restaurants and delis that will prepare food to go if you want to picnic; you may pick up snacks and cold drinks at many small markets scattered throughout the city.

GEOGRAPHY

Santa Barbara, the major city on California's Central Coast, has been described as the northernmost point in Southern California, the southernmost point of Northern California. Indeed, it's one of the few cities where the *Los Angeles Times* and *San Francisco Chronicle* are both widely available.

The south-facing beaches and east-west trending mountains of Santa Barbara create no end of confusion for would-be geographers. The sun sets not into the ocean, as it does throughout most of California, but behind the coastal range, which appears to be in the north. (Malibu is another spot with disorienting sunset.) A glance at the map is reassuring proof that the earth hasn't shifted on its axis.

ENTERTAINMENT

Santa Barbara has a number of first-run movie theaters where popular films can be viewed, along with two art film theaters, the Victoria and the Riviera.

For a comprehensive source of information about Santa Barbara's art and entertainment scene, pick up a copy of *The Independent,* a free weekly tabloid widely available at newsstands, news racks and shops along State Street. Published every Thursday, the paper includes critical reviews, listings of movies, nightclubs, lectures, meetings and the like, along with features about political and social issues.

The *Santa Barbara News-Press* is California's longest continuously published newspaper. Friday editions include "Scene Magazine," with news and reviews about local entertainment, artists and events.

THE LOBERO

CITY

Downtown
Santa Barbara
& Vicinity

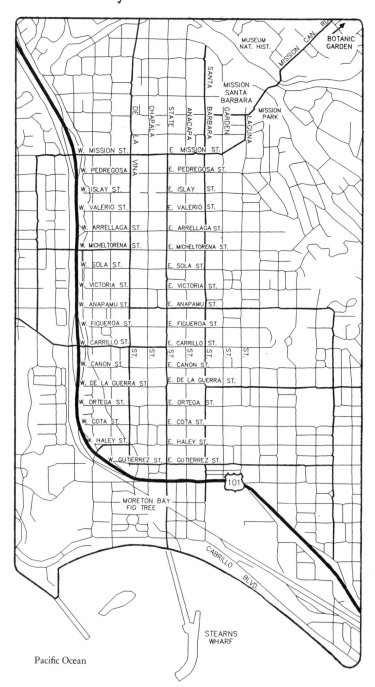

City

WHEN explorer Sebastián Vizcaino's crewmen found their tiny ship tossed about by a nasty storm on the eve of St. Barbara's Day in 1602, they prayed for her to intervene and save them from cruel death at sea. When the day dawned, and the ship found safe harbor, the grateful men named the spot for the saint.

Saint Barbara, whose father beheaded her after she embraced Christianity in defiance of his beliefs, symbolizes courage, faith and virtue to Christians all over the world. She is considered the patron saint of builders, architects and stonemasons, and is also believed to protect from sudden death due to natural disasters.

After the Presidio was founded as the military outpost to defend Spain's claim to this land, the Santa Barbara Mission was founded to enforce its religious rule. It was the tenth in the string of twenty-one missions founded along California's coast. After rejecting nearby Montecito as a Mission site—too many grizzlies and wolves—Mission Santa Barbara was consecrated on its present site on December 4, 1786, coinciding with the feast day of the martyred Saint Barbara.

THE MISSION: The first building was a rustic structure assembled of branches; it was replaced first with an adobe structure with a thatched roof, and that was replaced by a tile-topped adobe building that was destroyed in a massive earthquake in 1812. The stone edifice that stands today was begun in 1815, and was completed five years later. The earthquake of 1925 damaged the structure, but extensive and lengthy rebuilding efforts have successfully kept the "Queen of the Missions" in a remarkable state of repair. Few of California's missions have been so well-preserved.

Padre Antonio Ripoll designed the Mission, based on the designs of Vitruvius, a Roman architect who lived in the first century B.C., in the time of Caesar Augustus. Fr. Ripoll added a pair of Ionic columns along with the twin domed towers. The striking building is notable for its majestic dominance of the surrounding area. Gazing at it today, one can only imagine how it might have looked a century ago, when only fields, orchards and a dirt path shared the scene.

Thanks to the efforts of civic-minded folk, the Mission is still framed by plenty of open space, and the buildings that have been constructed nearby are in keeping with the elegance of the Mission's design. After the 1925 earthquake, the Mission Fathers were forced to sell land immediately south of the Mission to raise the money needed for repairs. Local citizens raised $35,000 to purchase the land, which is now Mission Historical Park. The large lawn has become a favorite spot for photography students, picknickers, lovers who stroll hand-in-hand, and visitors from all over the world. The rose garden contains a hundred species of roses, and their fragrance wafts on the warm summer breeze. Volunteers keep the roses healthy, but the lawn suffers during years of drought.

Of course, the Mission has always been more than just a church building. It represents the efforts of the Church to convert the native population to Christianity. This issue of the missionaries' treatment of the Indians is a somewhat ticklish subject even today. A Mission brochure reads, "The Franciscans did not own the mission. They administered the mission for the benefit of the Indians."

Whatever benefit they were providing—and the padres were no doubt convinced they were saving pagan Indians from an eternity of damnation—the Franciscan missionaries were determined to change the customs and religious beliefs of the hunter-gatherers they encountered in the New World. The two cultures obviously clashed.

Unwilling or unable to surrender their traditional ways and beliefs,

many Chumash died of stress and from exposure to European diseases. Besides relocating and changing their ways, the natives were also expected to provide the Missionary fathers with a free—if not always willing—source of labor. In addition to building the Mission itself, the Chumash helped construct the extensive aqueduct system and reservoirs that provided Santa Barbara with water. Forced to wear European-style clothing and live in houses, the Indians gave up hunting, fishing and gathering their food and began farming. Men learned to tend crops and cattle, make tiles and tan hides. Women were taught to spin wool, weave blankets and make tallow candles.

After California came under control of the Mexican government in the 1830s, Mission holdings were secularized, and some of the land was sold off. The Mission padres, however, continued their religious work.

The Indians were allowed to leave, but many of them had become dependent on the Mission and found themselves unable to return to their previous way of life. They could not afford to purchase land, nor did they have the experience to run ranchos when the Mission lands were carved up and sold. The Chumash population declined even more.

In 1839, the first bishop of Alta California selected the Santa Barbara Mission to become his home, thus ensuring that the site would not fall into disrepair—the fate that ruined many of California's missions.

Today, visitors come from all over the world to admire "the Queen of California Missions," examine the archival photos and artifacts, and read historic accounts of the purpose, intention and accomplishments of the Mission.

But the Mission is not just a tourist attraction; it serves as a worship site for an active parish community. A full schedule of masses are held, including an early morning weekday service that's a very special experience for the devout visitor. Dress appropriately, and maintain an attitude of reverence when visiting the Mission; it is, after all, a holy sanctuary.

1. Mission Santa Barbara, Museum of Natural History

HIGHLIGHTS: The Santa Barbara Mission is on every visitor's itinerary, and for good reason. The "Queen of California Missions," along with its exhibit hall, grounds and gardens, provides insights into California's earliest beginnings.

Not to be missed is the Mission's neighbor, the Santa Barbara Museum of Natural History, which offers an exploration of the human and natural history of Santa Barbara. Dioramas and displays orient the visitor to the natural environment—botanical, geological, oceanic, and more—and offer a hint of what the walker can experience by roaming the Santa Barbara coast and backcountry.

DISTANCE: A short walk, altogether less than a mile, but a long time on your feet.

INSIDER'S TIPS: The museum has vending machines stocked with snacks and soft drinks, but no meal facilities. Pack a lunch and plan a picnic at lovely Rocky Nook Park, located just a block from the museum. The oak-shaded park is studded with massive Mission Creek boulders; it's a great place for adults to relax, kids to play.

Mission Santa Barbara is open 9 A.M. to 5 P.M. daily; 1-5 P.M. on Sundays. Donation requested: $2 adults.

Santa Barbara Museum of Natural History is open 9 A.M. to 5 P.M. Monday through Saturday; 10 A.M. to 5 P.M. on Sunday. Admission charge for adults and children over 2; free admission on Family Sunday, the first Sunday of each month.

TRANSPORTATION: MTD bus to the Santa Barbara Mission. The bus also stops at the Museum of Natural History.

To reach the Mission by car, exit Highway 101 on Mission Street and head east to Laguna Street. Turn left and drive a few blocks to the Mission.

THE WALK: Take in the Mission's self-guided tour, which begins in the gift shop. You'll examine historic photos, interpretive proclamations, and a re-creation of a Franciscan padre's bedroom and the Mission kitchen.

You'll visit the Mission sanctuary, still in use today, as is the small chapel. Pause in the Sacred Garden to admire the succulents (the garden was closed to women visitors, except political wives and royalty, until 1959). Don't miss viewing the beautiful bell tower, which chimes melodically on the hour.

Cross the threshold, marked by a skull-and-crossbones, into the historic Mission cemetery. Among the vaults, plots and mausoleums are the remains of some 4,000 Indians and many prominent Santa Barbara families. Those familiar with the children's classic, *Island of the Blue Dolphins,* will notice a significant plaque on the wall. It marks the final resting place of the young woman, Juana Maria, who was known as "The Lost Woman of San Nicholas," and whose story was fictionalized in the book.

Exiting the cemetery and ending the Mission tour, look for twin sycamore trees standing nearby. As the legend goes, the trees were planted by sympathetic Mission Father O'Keefe to protect the Indian women from the sun as they took water from the aqueduct.

Admire the view from the Mission steps, and scout the adjacent asphalt parking lot for faded artwork. Every Memorial Day weekend, the parking lot becomes a painter's canvas as artists try their hand at the "I Madonnari" Street Painting Festival. The pastel coloring lasts until fall's first rains wash the chalk away.

Enjoy the whimsical sculpted bear heads of the lavendaria, where Indian women once laundered clothing. Over the years, the stone carvings on the bubbling Moorish fountain have been worn down by water and lime deposits.

Cross upper Laguna Street and head downhill over the wide lawn of the Mission to the rose garden located in Mission Historical Park. Species from all over the world are lovingly tended by volunteers; don't miss the picture-perfect view of the Mission framed by roses.

Following the sidewalk on the right (west side) of Laguna, then carefully crossing Alameda Padre Serra, take a look at the remains of stone structures built by the padres and the Chumash. The aqueduct, a

grist mill, pottery house and two reservoirs have survived several earthquakes and the ravages of time, and still stand among the pepper trees and palms.

Walk up Mission Canyon Road (a continuation of upper Laguna Street) to Rocky Nook Park. You'll pass a watering trough at the corner of Mountain Drive, placed here in memory of a former resident "who loved this cañon." Cross a handsome stone bridge over Mission Creek, and explore boulder-strewn and oak-studded Rocky Nook Park. It's an excellent picnic spot, and a good place to relax before taking in the Museum of Natural History.

"I can see that this museum has been built by the work of love," said Albert Einstein when he visited the Santa Barbara Museum of Natural History in 1931. It's an evaluation that pretty well sums up the efforts of uncounted volunteers, researchers and benefactors who have made the museum such a special place.

The marine exhibit alone is worth the trip; it's so complete one young visitor recently asked, "But where's the mermaid?" With stunning displays of a Robust Hooked Squid, a brilliant mural of the food web, and a fascinating wave machine, you'll learn plenty about Santa Barbara's offshore environment.

Bugs and birds, mammals and reptiles, rocks and flowers—all are displayed here with an emphasis on what can be found nearby.

Cultural exhibits provide an excellent perspective on the human occupation of this land. You'll view artifacts created by the Chumash people who once populated coastal Santa Barbara. Basketry and rock art, musical instruments and games, clothing and trading beads provide a glimpse of long-ago days.

The wooded museum grounds contain science classrooms, an education center, a planetarium, and a handsome stone amphitheatre. Field trips, lectures, workshps and volunteer programs are regularly sponsored by the museum. The museum gift shop has books and souvenir items.

If you're using the bus, catch it at the stop right out in front of the museum.

2. Santa Barbara Architecture

HIGHLIGHTS: A walk through some of Santa Barbara's most architecturally interesting neighborhoods. Enjoy a mix of Mission Revival, Victorian, Craftsman, and more modern designs.
DISTANCE: Two miles one-way.
INSIDER'S TIPS: Bob Easton, author of *Santa Barbara Architecture* (Capra Press, 1975, 1980), is a highly respected, highly opinionated architect and long-time resident of Santa Barbara. He devised this walk through several classic Santa Barbara neighborhoods, and offers an architectural historian's perspective on the buildings he considers among Santa Barbara's finest examples of Spanish Colonial Revival and of the Craftsman Movement. As Easton muses, "Architecture is history—use your imagination to bring it alive."
TRANSPORTATION: Take the MTD bus to the Mission. To reach the Mission by car, exit Highway 101 on Mission Street and head east to Laguna Street. Turn left and drive a few blocks to the Mission.

THE WALK: From the Mission steps, walk down to the fountain at the rose garden at Mission Historical Park. Pause a moment to admire the lovely block just in front of you—Plaza Rubio. It's a row of Spanish Colonial Revival homes designed by James Osborne Craig and Mary Craig, and built in the '20s.

The homes feature walled courtyards, simple arrangements and a sense of visual harmony. Architect Bob Easton notes, "The homes are absolute classics—nicely landscaped, there's a quiet, restful feeling about them. Allow your eye to wander and notice the details—iron gates, a lovely Spanish door, brick backyard patios."

After walking the length of Plaza Rubio and back, head across Laguna Street to the entrance of Junipero Plaza, marked by the the turn-of-the-century sandstone arches and iron gates. Proceed through

entrance to Junipero Plaza

the block to Garden Street, pausing to ponder the design at 333, and continue through the arches on Garden Street. Turn right, then make an almost immediate left on Los Olivos. Stop here, at 232 Los Olivos, to examine a fine home built by George Washington Smith, Santa Barbara's preeminent architect of the Spanish Colonial Revival style. Notice the fine details—the brick courtyard and walkway, iron gate and bougainvillea-draped wall.

Return to Garden Street, turning right, and heading toward downtown through one of Santa Barbara's great Upper Eastside neighborhoods. Note the hitching posts built from Santa Barbara sandstone.

Continue to a group of five homes located on a palm-lined section of Garden Street, from 2050 to 2010. Known as "Crocker Row," these were once vacation homes built by the Crocker family of San Francisco. Notice the window details and lovely Mission Revival style.

Look for the larger-than-life statue of the dog in front of the corner house at 2010, which is often the subject of speculation. It was placed there in the early 1900s in memory of a favorite pet left behind when the owners moved to California from Michigan. To the delight of many, the current residents often decorate it to coincide with holidays and special occasions. The dog has been seen wearing an Uncle Sam hat on the Fourth of July, a garland of flowers, and other holiday wear.

Continue down Garden, then turn left on Pedregosa to view the corner house of eclectic design—termed "Bavarian/Spanish" by our guide—then turn left on Laguna and examine the handsome bungalow at 1920 Laguna Street, representative of the Craftsman movement, circa 1910. Note the natural materials, low lines and rugged details, all characteristics of cottages like this one.

Return to Pedregosa, and continue heading east up the street, all the way past the DO NOT ENTER traffic sign. Turn right on Prospect for a view of a stunning house at 1741 Prospect. This beauty was built in 1911 by the noted architectural team of Greene and Greene, the only one of their houses built in Santa Barbara. The use of natural materials in the design is complemented by the landscaping and lovely gardens. Although it's partially hidden by shrubbery and built away from the street, it's worth craning your neck to get a good look. To examine this house from below, continue heading down Prospect (admire the view of the city below and the harbor beyond), and take a right on Valerio (note the sturdy stone garages), then a right on Olive Street where you'll hit the brick sidewalk. Look back up at the stately Greene and Greene design, and take in the natural beauty of this solid house and its graceful gardens, behind the Chinese archway.

Continue on the brick pathway, then turn left on Islay to view a number of cottage-style winter homes. Cross Laguna, staying on Islay as it jogs westward, then cross Garden Street, and turn left on Santa Barbara to 1721, to a most pleasing Victorian, a Queen Anne framed by two large palm trees.

Continue south along Santa Barbara Street to the corner of Santa Barbara and Valerio. Pause to look at the view—a real mixture of architectural styles. On one corner, you'll see a Byzantine-style Christian tower, a Spanish Colonial dome, and a Frank Lloyd Wright-inspired modern-looking Unitarian Church with towering coral trees.

Turn left on Valerio up to Garden Street, then turn right; at 1624 Garden note the curious apartment complex that looks like it's right out of one of the mystery novels written by the late, great Santa Barbara resident, Ross Macdonald.

At the corner of Arrellaga and Garden, pass through Alice Keck Park Memorial Garden, then turn right on Micheltorena. Stop at the corner to view another clash of styles; this time it's Our Lady of Sorrows Catholic Church situated behind the neo-classical bungalow office building, with the Arlington Theatre spire in the background.

At this point in the walk, you can either head downtown via Anacapa, or return to the Mission by improvising a route on Garden, Santa Barbara or Anacapa Streets to Mission Street. These mansion-lined streets give an impressive view of stately old Santa Barbara.

3. Santa Barbara Secrets

HIGHLIGHTS: On this walk, you'll visit a dream garden, pass a world-renowned resort and million-dollar mansions, discover a stairstep street, glimpse a hidden fountain and even walk along an Indian path. It's a walk you'll long remember, one that gives a very special view of Santa Barbara's best-kept secrets.

Your destination is the beautiful garden of Italian botanist Francesco Franceschi, but on this walk, the journey itself is as much a reward as the destination.

DISTANCE: A bit over 3 miles round trip. Don't get discouraged by the steep uphill at the beginning; the views and surprises are worth it.

INSIDER'S TIPS: This is most certainly should not be the first walk attempted by newly arrived visitors. Directions are a bit tricky, the possibility for getting lost greater than the other city walks in this guide. Late afternoon is a nice time for this saunter to secret places.

TRANSPORTATION: MTD bus to the Mission. To reach the Mission by car, exit Highway 101 on Mission Street and head east to Laguna Street. Turn left and drive a few blocks to the Mission.

NEARLY a century ago, Italian botanist Francesco Franceschi wrote, "One can live for years in Santa Barbara, and never get tired of admiring the scenery of the mountains that rise between us and the rest of the world." This hidden walk will reveal not only the lovely scenery of Santa Barbara, but several spots of special interest that remain virtually unknown, even to long-time residents.

We'll explain more, but not until you start walking!

THE WALK: From the Mission steps, cross the street to the MTD stop. Here you'll find a plaque commemorating the 1806 construction of the Mission aqueduct by the padres and the Chumash, as well as a length of the aqueduct itself.

Follow the sidewalk as it curves right onto Alameda Padre Serra (or APS as locals call it). A sign reads "Scenic Drive"; another, "El Encanto ½ mile." Stay with us, we'll lead you on a Scenic Walk to El Encanto—and to lots of places cars can't go.

At the sometimes busy and somewhat blind intersection of APS and Mission Canyon Road, cross APS to Mission Historical Park. Here you'll find the old Mission pottery building. Pick up the dirt path leading rightward and uphill past the old Mission reservoir site and a California Historical Landmark. Just steps away uphill is the Mission's grist mill and another reservoir site. Follow the dirt path as it leads upward through oak-, cactus- and brush-dotted slopes. Crosses atop churches and the tops of palms dominate the skyline from this point of view.

The path soon intersects a stone staircase. A right down the stairs leads back to APS, but you head left, climbing a few stairs to Mission Ridge Road. Walk 50 yards to the signed intersection of Mission Ridge Road and Mission Ridge Lane, staying left on the former road and beginning an ascent past some lovely Mediterranean-style homes.

The Riviera, one of Santa Barbara's most beautiful spots, affords grand views of the city, harbor and Channel Islands beyond. When a state community college campus was established on the Riviera in 1909, a number of large homes were built; gardens were planted, a streetcar line was established and immigrant stonemasons were hired to fashion the local stone into the walls, hitching posts and stairsteps that remain to this day.

Continuing on your walk, you'll pass Marymount School on your left, Brooks Institute of Photography, and the Riviera office complex on your right. At the corner of Alvarado Place and Mission Ridge is the El Encanto Hotel; visit it on your return.

Continue just above the El Encanto, smug with the satisfaction of knowing that you've already completed more than half the climb. About when the houses run out, examine the grand view to your right, and beyond the eucalyptus trees to your left, the redwood home of Dr. Francesco Franceschi. Now, something more mundane: a series of metal and cement guardrails, then a stairwell. Opposite the stairwell is a sign reading "Rock Slide Area," and up above, the Franceschi home.

Keep following Mission Ridge Road to 1510 on your left. Don't turn up the private drive, but pick up the trail at a multi-trunked eucalyptus, and the Franceschi Park sign, zigzagging up-slope through the gardens.

The 14-acre park site is all that remains of the 40 acres purchased by Dr. Emanual Orazio Fenzi, a horticulturist who moved here from his native Florence, Italy in 1893. He changed his name to Francesco Franceschi, built the redwood house which he dubbed "Montarioso" (airy mountain), and dreamt of establishing a model botanic garden on the then-barren, boulder-strewn spot. Although his grand plans fell somewhat short, he managed to introduce some 330 species to the area, and identified and catalogued 600 native species. He is perhaps best remembered as the man who introduced the zucchini to America.

Civic leader Pearl Chase was instrumental in preserving the mansion and establishing the park; today's restoration efforts are being led by the Santa Barbara County Horticultural Society and the Friends of Franceschi.

After you've enjoyed the park, return to Mission Ridge Road and descend to 1445, then follow the guardrail a hundred feet to a stone staircase, descending it to a cement walkway that heads south/southeast. This path soon splits; the left fork tunnels under oaks, but you turn right and continue downhill. Stop a moment to enjoy commanding views of the harbor and the city. Continue on the stone stairway and descend to Dover Road.

Go right on Dover a short block to a three-way junction. The upper road, Lasuen, leads to El Encanto; the middle road dead-ends in a lovely landscaped turnaround. You descend on Paterna Road, walking on the sidewalk on the right side of the street past stone walls and admiring the lovely homes. Paterna Road meets and joins Lasuen, and you continue on the latter road. You'll soon spy the red sidewalk leading up to El Encanto Hotel.

The red sidewalk climbs to the entrance of El Encanto. Read the words by Henry Van Dyke on a sign above the door:

*The lintel low enough to keep out pomp and pride. The
threshold high enough to turn deceit aside; the doorband
strong enough from robbers to defend, This door will
open at a touch to welcome every friend.*

Either continue along Lasuen a short block, or descend from the
entrance of El Encanto to the corner of Lasuen and Alvarado. Join the
asphalt path that leads diagonally to Riviera Park Research and
Communication Center. Here you'll find a colonnade and a courtyard
with a beautiful pool. At the end of the Riviera complex is the Riviera
Theatre. Notice the Chumash sculpture: a man with a pipe, a woman
grinding acorns in a bowl, as well as two shields, one with an ax, one
with an arrow.

From the Riviera Theatre, take the stairs to the lower parking lot,
then cut across the lot to the exit at APS. Cross APS to the sidewalk,
turn right, and walk 100 feet, looking left for a concrete stairway with
steel pipe handrails. Descend the stairs, follow a cement path, then
drop down another dozen stairs to short, steep Sierra Street, which
might just as well be located in San Francisco, judging from its incline.
Enjoy the neighborhood, and head for the end of the street at Grand.
Go right. Almost immediately, at Oreña Street, Grand splits. Take the
lower road to its end at Plaza Bonita, where a Mission Revival
neighborhood surrounds a restful fountain complete with fish pond,
waterlilies, and stone benches.

Double-back a few steps to Oreña, and head down two short, steep
blocks to Emerson Avenue. Go right one-half block to Padre. You can
see Mission Historical Park, but don't head for it just yet; one more
secret awaits your discovery.

Turn left on Padre, walking the sidewalk on the right side of the
street. Look right, between 421 and 417 Padre Street, for the secret
public paseo. Local legend has it that this passageway was part of an
Indian pathway that led from the Mission to the Presidio. The path
ends at Plaza Rubio, bringing you face-to-face with the fountain and
the rose garden in the foreground, the Mission in the background.
Linger awhile to savor the garden, then head back to the Mission.

4. Santa Barbara Botanic Garden

HIGHLIGHTS: A quiet corner of Santa Barbara, nestled in the rugged landscape of Mission Canyon, the Santa Barbara Botanic Garden is truly a treasure, a living museum. Miles of soft pathways leading through California's ecosystems allow quick getaways from city life. The garden, home to more than 1,000 species of native trees, shrubs, flowers and grasses, is a place to linger and learn.

DISTANCE: It's only about a mile walk around the garden, up to 5½ miles if you explore all of the garden's side trails. Those hikers looking for some serious exercise can explore the upper reaches of Mission Canyon, Seven Falls and Inspiration Point via Tunnel Trail. (See Walk #30)

INSIDER'S TIPS: Docent-led nature walks daily at 2 P.M.; 10:30 A.M. on Saturday and Sunday. Many special events scheduled throughout the year.

TRANSPORTATION: (Alas, city bus service does not extend to the botanic garden.) From U.S. 101 in Santa Barbara, exit on Mission Street and head east to Laguna Street. Turn left and keeping the Santa Barbara Mission on your left, you'll soon join Mission Canyon Road. When you reach a stop sign at Foothill Road, turn right, then make an almost immediate left back onto Mission Canyon Road. At a distinct V-intersection, keep right on Mission Canyon Road and follow it nearly to road's end, where you'll find the Santa Barbara Botanic Garden. Park in the garden's lot.

Hours are 9 A.M. to sunset daily; bookshop 9-5.

Admission charges Thursday through Monday: Adults $3; seniors and teens $2; children 5-12 $1; maximum charge per family $8.

FOUNDED in 1926, this enclave devoted to the display, protection and research of native species has grown from its original 13 acres to its present size of 65 acres. Ecosystems represented include meadow, desert, chaparral, woodland, arroyo, and several others. This is one of the few locations in Southern California where a coast redwood forest has been successfully planted. These magnificent trees, located on the flat streambed along Mission Creek, provide a shady retreat with their canopied limbs and massive trunks.

The many floral life zones provide shelter for a number of species of wildlife, among them several dozen birds, amphibians and reptiles. Keep your eyes open for mammals, ranging from the California pocket mouse to mule deer.

Among the ongoing programs offered by the garden are lectures, docent-led tours, field trips to other gardens, classes and workshops. The extensive research facilities include an herbarium, library, well-stocked garden bookshop, year-round nursery and twice-yearly plant sales.

THE WALK: From the garden's main entrance, as you pass the entrance kiosk and approach the bookstore, turn left on the path and head down into Mission Canyon. The buckwheat-bedecked trail descends into an arroyo ecosystem full of toyon and lemonade berry. Side trails lead to the garden's manzanita section.

California Lilac

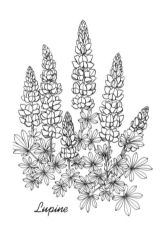

Lupine

Bigleaf Maple

The trail drops to the bottom of Mission Canyon, crosses Mission Creek and reaches an intersection with Easton Trail. Follow the Easton Trail as it climbs moderately up the west wall of the canyon. Watch for some pieces of adobe pipe; these 200-year-old remnants of the Santa Barbara Mission waterworks system, unearthed when the Easton Trail was built.

Easton Trail descends to the garden's island section. Here you can marvel at the wonders of evolution, at how Channel Islands plant species have evolved differently than their mainland cousins.

Joining Canyon Trail, you'll proceed up Mission Canyon, which is no planted garden, but a natural oak-sycamore woodland that was thriving long before Europeans arrived at California's shores.

The trail crosses over the top of Mission Creek Dam, built to hold water for the padres, Spanish soldiers and Indian converts. From the dam, a trail loops around a redwood grove. Planted 50 years ago, the redwoods are doing nicely in the cool canyon.

Now join one of the trails ascending out of the canyon to the main part of the garden. Enjoy the wide meadow and its multitude of flora with identification tags and Latin names, then make your way back to the garden's bookstore and trailhead.

Woolly Blue-curls

5. State Street

HIGHLIGHTS: State Street has historically been the major corridor of commerce in Santa Barbara. Banks, medical buildings, hotels and shopping areas have been clustered on the street for more than a century. Today, the number of attractive shops, inviting ambience, and the historic feel, attract shoppers and strollers from around the world to this street.

DISTANCE: Eight blocks one way.

TRANSPORTATION: Downtown/Waterfront Shuttle. Begin at the Arlington Theatre, 1317 State St.

INSIDER'S TIPS: The Arlington Theatre, where this walk begins, houses a magnificent pipe organ that has been restored by a group of hard-working volunteers. The Santa Barbara Theatre Organ Society sponsors an annual concert series; inquire at the Arlington ticket agency.

STRETCHING the length of the city, State Street—Santa Barbara's Main Street—has different moods at different times of the day. On cool mornings, a stroll down the shady street reveals the city just waking up. Traffic is light; sidewalk cafés, muffin shops and bakeries serve up their best cuppa java to early-rising tourists and impatient commuters; shop owners sweep the sidewalk and tidy their storefronts. Only the whine of the gardeners' leaf blowers disturb the tranquility of the morning.

By mid-afternoon, the street bustles in the bright sunlight. The air filled with a dozen different languages as visitors shop the day away.

In the evenings, diners and film-goers replace shoppers on the

sidewalk. Theatres turn on their neon signs, and the whole street takes on new life. Restaurants open their doors, and the hippest clubs in town attract decked-out dancers for a night-on-the-town. The street becomes a cruise strip, music blares from car stereos, and everybody checks out everybody else.

Open-air shopping paseos on State Street include Victoria Court, La Arcada, San Marcos and El Paseo, which offer an array of unique shops; goods range from tourist T-shirts to one-of-a-kind art objects. Restaurants within strolling distance offer diverse dining experiences—everything from Tex-Mex to California Cuisine, from funky coffeehouse fare to elegant gourmet meals.

Downtown State Street—not to be confused with upper State Street, which has a commercial district and motel row of its own, or with lower State Street, sometimes called Old Town—is the commercial heart of the city, an interesting mix of old and new. It's still possible to discover some Mom-and-Pop shops, but rising rents and redevelopment are forcing many to relocate or go out of business altogether. Some bemoan the loss of distinctive historic buildings and small businesses, while others advocate modernization as necessary for the city's economic health. Without a doubt, State Street is changing and at a much more rapid pace than ever before. Time will tell if the street will keep its charm, or grow to resemble the mini-malled and overdeveloped shopping strips of suburban Los Angeles. One very popular Santa Barbara restaurant and watering hole, The Chase seems to be covering its bets: it has locations on upper State, downtown, and an additional one on lower State.

THE WALK: The Arlington Theatre is an architectural gem. Built in the early 1930s on the site of the old Arlington Hotel, it is an excellent example of Spanish Colonial Revival design, created by architect Joseph Plunkett. The murals on the walls, tile work, graceful columns, wrought-iron details and heavy, painted beams combine to give this building a Mediterranean style; it was designated a city landmark in 1975.

In a world of mall theaters that are little more than warehouses with screens, it's a pleasure to view a movie or attend a concert staged in this grand picture palace with its distinctive spire-topped roof. Inside, make-believe stars twinkle on the curved ceiling above an extravagantly decorated performance house that resembles a Mediterranean village.

Head downtown (south) on State Street, and turn right on Victoria to see a large tile mural applied to the side of a building that houses a supermarket. The mural depicts Santa Barbara County history from Chumash culture to the Space Age.

Head back to State and wander into Victoria Court. Several shops, restaurants and services are offered along the street and within the winding paths and courtyards.

Several shops, restaurants and services are offered along the street and within the winding paths and courtyards.

Note the Granada Building on the east side of State; it's an eight-story office building and theater complex. It was constructed without windows on three sides, because developers fully expected that one day State Street would be lined with similar such high-rises. But that was just before the devastating 1925 earthquake, and the subsequent action by the City Council banning all commercial buildings above four stories high. So the Granada remains the tallest building in Santa Barbara, and one of the few that wasn't heavily damaged in the earthquake. Judge for yourself if you think the Granada is distinctive-looking or merely sticks out like a sore thumb.

Located in the 1100 block of State Street are the former Woolworth Building, which housed the local five-and-dime until the late 1980s, and the San Marcos building, built in 1869 to serve as the city's first secondary school. It was later converted into a hotel and today it houses an array of shops, restaurants and offices.

During the 1925 earthquake, the San Marcos lost its two top floors but the lower floors survived intact. The ornamental facade was added after the quake. Stroll into the paseo to enjoy a bit of old California.

The Santa Barbara Museum of Art's proud building, located at State and Anapamu, formerly housed the city's post office; it was converted in the thirties, then remodeled in 1983. It's a handsome building, best seen from across the street to fully appreciate the classic Italian design and effective landscaping that seems to form its base. The Art Museum gives way to La Arcada Court, a popular paseo that features tempting restaurants and a collection of art galleries and lovely shops. The cast dolphins, located within the arcade, are popular with parents who like to photograph their children sitting atop them. They were created by local artist Bud Bottoms, who also designed the dolphin statue located at the foot of Stearns Wharf.

At 1029 State Street, two plaques mark the changing face of the spot. Located here first was an adobe owned by the Orella family; in 1927, the Copper Coffee Pot was built. Another restaurant has taken over the building and modified it somewhat, but the lovely balcony and patio area still remain.

Continue strolling down State Street, visiting the shops that suit your fancy, noting the many examples of Colonial Revival architecture—with red-tiled roofs, arches, wrought-iron details, the use of Greek columns, colorful awnings, and second-floor balconies.

El Paseo, designed by architect James Osborne Craig, is a cluster of small shops, offices and cafe situated next to the historic Casa de la Guerra. Wander "The Street of Spain" and note the red-tiled roofs, white walls and classic iron grillwork, tiles, landscaping, and beautiful fountain.

Storke Placita at 722 State Street is named for the founder and editor of the *Santa Barbara News-Press,* Thomas Storke. A statue of King Carlos III was removed after it was repeatedly and irreverently decorated by the homeless and Bohemian folks who once frequented the plaza. Outraged locals complained long and loud enough to convince city officials a re-vamp of the once-tiny plaza was high-priority. During the height of the recession, the sum of $250,000 was spent to spruce up the spot. The original architectural plans called for old King Carlos to be re-placed atop the fountain that now occupies the plaza, but another brouhaha developed over the symbolism of the Spanish king, and he was installed instead in a compromise location near the Presidio.

But nobody seems to be happy with the way the place looks today. The very red tile, the huge chain that encircles the still-topless fountain, the tiny little globe lamps . . . the list goes on. But it gives people something to talk about, and the homeless have been replaced by teens and twentysomethings who hang out daily in the plaza, a place that now has a story bigger than the space it occupies.

Anchoring the State Street Stroll is Paseo Nuevo, a development of upscale chain stores, boutique shops and restaurants, as well as a theater complex, performing arts center and museum of contemporary art.

6. Paseo Santa Barbara

HIGHLIGHTS: A leisurely stroll of Santa Barbara's scenic paseos. Offers off-the-beaten-path views of Santa Barbara, through unique shopping areas, past restaurants, and historical sites. The fun—and challenge—is to use the city's paseos, not State, Anacapa or Chapala streets, except when absolutely necessary.

DISTANCE: Fourteen blocks round trip.

INSIDER'S TIPS: Use caution in parking lots and when crossing streets.

TRANSPORTATION: Downtown/Waterfront Shuttle.

If you're arriving by car, park in the city lot on Ortega, between State Street and Anacapa Street.

IT'S no accident that Santa Barbara is so easily accessible on foot; the city has been carefully designed with the pedestrian in mind. The tradition dates back to the Presidio days, and it continues more than two centuries later.

The term *paseo* refers to a pedestrian lane or walkway. Since the area has been extensively redeveloped in recent years, city agencies have attempted to continue the tradition of the paseos, even with the addition of multi-level city parking lots.

The most attractive paseos are graceful, charming and romantic, lined with lovely gardens, interesting shops and outdoor cafes. Others, however, are little more than alleyways, obviously requiring attention before they can properly be termed paseos. But taken as a whole, the paseo system of walkways gives a human-sized quality and dimension to Santa Barbara's downtown streets.

THE WALK: Our paseo walk begins on the north side of Ortega street, between the News-Press Building and the interesting building

[46]

at the corner of Anacapa and Ortega, long-ago site of the County Courthouse. Walk through the News-Press parking lot past the loading dock, and angle left toward the flower beds to de la Guerra Plaza Street, the tiny street that borders historic de la Guerra Plaza.

Since the early 1800s, de la Guerra Plaza has been Santa Barbara's ceremonial gathering spot and festival site. Each year, during the city's Old Spanish Days celebration, the plaza becomes a *mercado,* or marketplace.

The News-Press Building that anchors the plaza was designed by architect George Washington Smith in 1922. The newspaper, now owned by the *New York Times,* is the oldest daily journal published in Southern California. A number of distinctive shops and restaurants line the perimeter of the plaza.

Also located on de la Guerra Plaza is Santa Barbara's City Hall, a small, graceful building of Spanish Colonial Revival style. Built in 1923, it somehow survived the 1925 earthquake, and served as a model during the city's rebuilding efforts. Today, it's a common sight to view news crews as they set up their taping sessions and interview city officials in front of the building.

From the east side of plaza, cross de la Guerra Street, and head across to "the Street in Spain" in lovely El Paseo. This is the gateway to one of Santa Barbara's most unique and historic spots: wander the narrow walkways, peaceful courtyard and interesting collection of shops, art galleries and studios. Stop awhile at one of the charming outdoor cafés; enjoy the burbling fountain and beautiful gardens in the Mediterranean setting.

Be sure to examine the tiles that tell the story of Santa Barbara, and visit Casa de la Guerra museum and shop, where you may look at interesting vintage photos of de la Guerra family, and early views of Santa Barbara's first mansion. This was the site of the grand fandango (the wedding celebration of the youngest de la Guerra daughter) that Richard Henry Dana wrote about in *Two Years Before the Mast.*

As you make your way through the labyrinthine corridors, you'll end up in the parking lot across the street from the post office. In front of you is the tiny building occupied by Madame Rosinka the Palm Reader. Head over to the paseo located between El Centro Building and the west side of the Lobero Theatre. Check the coming attractions kiosk, and then walk along the brick walkway where a red hibiscus blooms delightfully during the summer months. Follow the beige tiles, then angle west (left) behind Santa Barbara Bank and Trust and the Masonic Temple. Curving right, you'll emerge between a Spanish-style row of shops and the Bank of Montecito, coming face-to-face with a lovely Monterey Revival-style building, and its next-door neighbor, the Hill-Carrillo Adobe on Carrillo Street. Cross the street; from this vantage point, look back at the ornate Mediterranean designs on the Masonic Temple.

Visit the Hill-Carrillo Adobe (open Tuesday through Friday 12 P.M. to 4 P.M.), then return to the paseo walk. Walk along the eastern (right) side of the adobe, keep on a northward path, and head past a row of junipers. Ascend the stairsteps leftward, then continue north behind the restaurants and shops. Pause at the sycamore-shaded benches to examine the view. You'll spot distinctive buildings with red-tiled roofs, palm trees, and the Santa Ynez mountains in the distance. The sharp-eyed will note the Courthouse tower.

Cross Figueroa Street, jog to the right just a bit and head into La Arcada. Inside, enjoy the casual ambience of this classic paseo, its fountains, flower pots, bright flags and tiles. Linger awhile at the shops, art galleries and outdoor eateries.

Walk past the back entrance of the Museum of Art, alongside the Main Library, where you'll examine the abstract sculpture of lacquered steel entitled *Intermezzo* by Anthony Caro. Walk between the museum and the library toward Anapamu Street, cross the street and head a few steps to the right. Pass through the bougainvillea-draped walkway across Anapamu Street, skirting the parking lot and bearing left, angling toward two ersatz Corinthian columns, and turning left to State Street.

(Do note that the return trip of the paseo walk is a little more challenging than the first half, but be dogged. The city has not been as

El Paseo Courtyard

faithful to the paseo concept on the west side of State Street as it has been on the east. The persistent paseo walker must twice detour to Chapala Street.)

Cross State Street, heading right into Victoria Court, where you'll explore shops and restaurants, and a pleasant ambience—even the McDonald's was done in Mission Revival style. (Oh, how to put this delicately . . . Victoria Court is the location of the only pay toilets we've ever seen in Santa Barbara. A quarter buys relief for the long-distance walker.)

Walk to the back of Victoria Court, to the sidewalk fronting the parking lot and turn left by the tiny post office. Stay on the paseo to Anapamu Street; turn right to examine the wall that hides the parking lot. It offers two points of interest: a snoozing cat sculpture and a tile mural explaining the meaning of the Chumash word *anapamu*.

Cross Anapamu Street. When the Karpeles Manuscript Library is open (Wednesday through Sunday 1 P.M. to 4 P.M.), stop in and examine its priceless letters and documents penned by historic figures including Napoleon, George Washington, Albert Einstein, Abraham Lincoln and King Henry VIII. When the library is open, continue straight through to the next paseo; if closed, head right to Chapala Street at Anapamu, then make the first left back into the parking lot.

Pass through Paseo Figueroa, then a parking lot with the Transit Center on your right. The paseo ends again at Carrillo; head right to Chapala, then left and left again into the bricked parking lot and paseo. Don't miss the tile compass embedded in the walkway. Re-orient yourself and head eastward, noting the elaborate parking structure on the right, the nicely landscaped storefronts on the left.

Crossing Canon Perdido, you'll enter Santa Barbara's newest shopping area, Paseo Nuevo. In the mix of specialty shops and architectural details between Nordstrom and The Broadway, don't miss the new home of the Santa Barbara Contemporary Arts Forum.

To get there, take a right just past the large semi-circular gathering place and twin fountains. Head toward Chapala Street, then ascend the tiled, multi-pattern Grand Staircase (you could take the elevator, but, hey, you're a walker). At the top of the stairs, head right into the 4,600-square-foot forum, which houses two exhibit spaces, a media library, shop and bookstore.

Across the way from CAF is the Center Stage Theater, a state-of-the-art, community-access theatre that offers flexible seating arrangements for audiences up to 150. Check the box office for a schedule of performances.

Head back down the stairs, then meander through Paseo Nuevo to Ortega Street, and your starting point.

7. Santa Barbara History and Culture

HIGHLIGHTS: You'll explore the exotic Santa Barbara County Courthouse, tour some of the first dwellings and structures in town, and visit several culturally significant sites, including a historic performing arts center, the Historical Museum, the public library with its art gallery, and the famed Museum of Art. Along the way, you'll have the chance to stop in lovely courtyards and stop to eat at any number of tempting restaurants.

DISTANCE: Not much more than a mile, but plan to spend the better part of a morning or afternoon; this is a walk that demands lots of time and attention.

TRANSPORTATION: Downtown/Waterfront Shuttle to Anapamu Street; walk two blocks east to the Courthouse.

This walk begins at the Santa Barbara County Courthouse, which occupies the entire 1100 block of Anacapa Street. Parking is available on the street (90-minute zone strictly enforced) or in the lot just behind the public library. Enter via Anacapa opposite the courthouse.

INSIDER'S TIPS: Free admission to the Santa Barbara County Courthouse daily; docent-led tours Tuesday through Saturday at 2; additional tours Wednesday and Friday at 10:30 A.M.; the observation tower closes at 4:45. P.M.

Free admission to the Santa Barbara Museum of Art every Thursday and the first Sunday of the month; closed on Monday; open Tuesday through Saturday 11 A.M. to 5 P.M., Thursday 11 A.M. to 9 P.M., Sunday noon to 5 P.M.

Historical Museum closed on Monday, open Tuesday through Saturday 10 A.M. to 5 P.M., Sunday 12 noon to 5 P.M.; free docent-led tours Wednesday, Saturday and Sunday at 1:30 P.M.; Gledhill Library open Tuesday through Friday 10 A.M. to 4 P.M.

SANTA BARBARA COURTHOUSE

THE WALK: The huge, gleaming white stucco building topped with a red tile roof is one of the most distinctive public structures in America. Visitors sometimes fail to realize that the Santa Barbara County Courthouse is not just a tourist attraction, but the building where all manner of government business takes place. As you wander through the tile- and wrought iron-adorned hallways, remember that marriage licenses and birth certificates are obtained here, grand juries assembled, voters registered, bankruptcies declared, arraignments held and prisoners sentenced.

The courthouse is an example of Spanish Colonial Revival architecture; it was built after the 1925 earthquake destroyed the previous masonry structure located on the same site. San Francisco architect William Mooser and his son were awarded the contract for the replacement building. The younger Mooser had lived in Spain and studied Moorish design; his background obviously influenced this project.

Before entering the building on Anacapa Street, note the lovely stone fountain entitled *The Spirit of the Ocean.* Then head through the arch, where inscribed into the sandstone is: DIOS NOS DIO LOS CAMPOS EL ARTE HUMANA EDIFICO CIUDADES, which translates to: "God Gave Us the Country the Skill of Man Hath Built the Town." The medallions of Industry and Agriculture are positioned below.

Time your visit to take a docent-led tour, or wander through the hallways on your own. Notice the grand ceiling design just above this entrance; it's a replica of one seen in a synagogue in Toledo, Spain. Be sure to stop in the second-floor mural room for an artistic overview of Santa Barbara history.

For the best view in town, head for the clock tower, El Mirador (take the elevator to the fourth floor). This observation deck, 85 feet above ground, gives you a panoramic view of the entire city. Compass points painted on the floor help visitors get oriented with Santa Barbara's sometimes confusing layout.

SANTA BARBARA
COURTHOUSE

To the northwest, see the lovely twin-towered Mission; to the north, the majestic Santa Ynez mountains that form the backdrop for the city. East and southwest views are of the ocean and palm-lined Cabrillo Avenue.

Head back down to the first floor, exit the courthouse and stroll around the grounds. You'll find arches carved with quotations from Virgil (LEARN JUSTICE FROM THIS WARNING) and Coke (REASON IS THE LIFE OF THE LAW), tile murals—including one commemorating the visit of Queen Elizabeth and Prince Philip in 1983—and the so-called sunken garden, which is planted on the foundation area of the former courthouse building. The amphitheatre is the site for annual summer celebrations, including an Independence Day concert and performances during the city's Fiesta Days.

After strolling the grounds, make your way to Santa Barbara Street (parallel to Anacapa, the street behind the main Courthouse entrance) and head south to continue the walk.

Stop at the tile plaque on the modern building at 1014 Santa Barbara Street. It's the former site of the Koury Market, a neighborhood market that was the "Home of the five-cent sandwich."

Continue one more block down Santa Barbara Street to Canon Perdido and turn right. Here you'll find the next stop on the walk, El Presidio de Santa Barbara State Historic Park. The one-time Spanish military fortress was founded here in 1782, one of four such outposts in California, and is currently under reconstruction based on archeological excavations that have been conducted on the Presidio site since the mid-60s.

Don't miss the fifteen-minute slide show that documents the Spanish colonization of the area two centuries ago, up to the present-day restoration efforts. Take a stroll through El Presidio Chapel, a re-creation of the city's first church. The Spanish artifacts on the altar and colorful wall paintings provide an interesting contrast to the building's simple exterior.

Stop in the park headquarters to view a display of artifacts found on the Presidio site, and to read about the history of the Canedo Adobe, the former quarters for military officers, a private home, and even a Chinese laundry. The Santa Barbara Trust for Historic Preservation, now headquartered here, is responsible for the reconstruction and interpretation of the Presidio. In 1987, the organization was the national winner of the "Take Pride in America Award."

The Presidio was built on a different grid than the one that Santa Barbara is now built on, so it's a bit difficult to visualize how it might have originally looked. The quadrangle, consisting of Presidio buildings, defense walls and bastions actually take up portions of four city blocks. Eventually, the Trust hopes to finish the reconstruction project, and has purchased many properties in the Presidio quadrangle.

Workers recently completed a new wing adjacent to the chapel, and could be seen making the mud-and-straw adobe bricks that were used in the construction.

To continue the walk, keep heading south down Santa Barbara Street, stopping at the Rochin Adobe, the first parcel of land sold after the Presidio was dismantled. Anyone who has the slightest knowledge about Santa Barbara real estate prices will be astonished to know that the 1856 selling price of this 250-foot by 120-foot lot was originally $30. The house, which is privately owned and currently inhabited by descendants of the original family, is constructed of adobe bricks salvaged from the Presidio wall; painted wooden siding obscures the adobe, however.

At the corner of Santa Barbara Street and de la Guerra, stop in at the Santa Barbara Historical Museum. An original gas lamp that once stood on State Street is installed in the front of the museum. This eclectic collection of Santa Barbara/California memorabilia includes artists' renderings of Missions and Santa Barbara buildings, a nineteenth-century wicker pony cart, a sacred Chinese shrine that was once a part of Santa Barbara's Chinatown, and sketches by Edward Borein, a renowned Western artist. The focus of one display is a Santa Barbara map, circa 1886; it's fun to try to conjure up an image of what the small town looked like back then.

A poem about Santa Barbara is inscribed on the map:

> *Where falls no hail . . . not any snow,*
> *Nor ever wind blows loudly, but it lies*
> *Deep meadow'd, happy, fair, with orchard-lawns*
> *And bowery hollows, crowned with summer-sea.*

The museum's research library, Gledhill Library, is located in the lovely courtyard area behind the museum. Its extensive collection of books, maps, photographs, genealogy charts, documents and oral history tapes is available to researchers. Historic photos on display provide a wondrous glimpse into Santa Barbara's past.

The walk continues on Santa Barbara Street, at the quiet grounds and lovely gardens of Casa Covarrubias, a historic adobe built for early Santa Barbara leaders in 1817. Today, the house, which has been designated a California Historic Landmark, serves as headquarters for Los Rancheros Visitadores.

Retrace your steps on Santa Barbara Street back to de la Guerra Street (in front of and then west of the Historical Museum). Note the tiles on buildings across the street that indicate the site of the original Presidio, and pause at 112-116 de la Guerra to view the lovely Mediterranean courtyard of the Meridian Studios. The stucco and brick studios were built in 1923 by the noted architect George Washington Smith. The historic Lugo adobe, built about 1830, stands at the end of the courtyard. Behind the wrought iron gate stand a cherub statue surrounded by ferns and a hibiscus often in bloom with bright red flowers. The offices located in this tranquil setting house a number of artists engaged in various professions.

Cross the street to tiny Presidio Avenue, the oldest street in Santa Barbara. This is the site of the Guardhouse, commemorated by a tile plaque. Around the corner, read the framed proclamation of El Adobe de Miranda, once occupied by Captain John C. Frémont who was called to Santa Barbara to quell a revolt by Mission Indians. Just across the way, stop at Presidio Gardens, the peaceful courtyard surrounded by law offices. With its koi pond, fountain and shaded gardens, it's a perfect spot for a rest or even a picnic lunch. Don't miss the graceful blue vases that stand atop the building outside the courtyard.

Return to de la Guerra, named for the first commandante of the Presidio, and turn right on Anacapa Street. You'll pass historic El Paseo shopping and dining area (see Walk #6) on your left and the tempting outdoor café on your right. Continue north on Anacapa, past the post office on your right. A commemorative marker noting the establishment of the Presidio on the site has been presented and placed at the top of the stairs by the Native Sons of the American

West. The post office was built in 1937; its Art Deco design, with a Spanish influence, combine to make it a distinctive building.

Note the Lobero Theatre building at the corner of Canon Perdido and Anacapa. It is the second performing arts forum to stand on this site.

In 1873, Italian immigrant Giuseppe "José" Lobero, realized his dream of building a grand opera house to rival those in his native land. Despite the fact that the theatre stood in what at the time was considered a bad side of town, the 1,300-seat opera house flourished for more than a decade. But a small town like Santa Barbara could hardly support such an entertainment palace; it fell on hard times and eventual foreclosure. Lobero finally committed suicide in 1892, and the building was razed in 1922.

Local citizens raised nearly $200,000 to build a new theater, which opened in 1924. Miraculously, it was not damaged in the 1925 earthquake that devastated much of the city. In the years since its opening, the theater has hosted Hollywood's top stars. Today, the non-profit Lobero Theatre Foundation manages the theater and hosts an array of performing artists from all over the world. The 600-seat Lobero is noted for its intimacy and elegant surroundings. Stop by the ticket office and check out the performance schedule.

Head back up Anacapa, noting the Courthouse clock tower on the right just a few blocks away. Stop to admire the four-story Lobero Building at 924 Anacapa; it was designed by noted San Francisco architect Julia Morgan, who is known for her work on the magnificent Hearst Castle. She also designed the ivy-covered brick Community Recreation Center building next door.

At this point in the walk, you have an option of returning to the Courthouse, or continuing on to the art galleries of the public library and the Santa Barbara Museum of Art.

At the corner of Anacapa and Anapamu stands the Santa Barbara Public Library. Head west on Anapamu to the entrance, stopping first to admire the decorative arch that was once the main doorway. The figures are Aristotle and Plato; the crests surrounding the city's coat of arms are the shields of four of the world's great libraries: University of Bologna (Italy), Bibliothèque Nationale (France), University of Salamanca (Spain) and Oxford's Bodleian Library (England). Inside

the library, the Faulkner Gallery showcases the work of local artists.

Continue west on Anapamu to State Street, turn left, and head up the steps to the Santa Barbara Museum of Art.

The museum houses the most extensive collection of art on the Central Coast. Whether your tastes run to antiquities, Asian art, French impressionism, or abstract expressionism, you're sure to find something you like in this impressive regional museum. Among the treasures in the permanent collection are *Brooklyn Bridge* #7 by David Hockney and *Kneeling Caryatid* by Auguste Rodin.

Gallery tours, talks and special lecture series are regularly scheduled, as are classes and workshops for children and very popular art tours of destinations as diverse as Santa Fe, Moscow and Istanbul. The museum bookstore features an interesting collection of art books, jewelry and gift items.

Return to the Courthouse by heading east on Anapamu.

8. Old Town to the Ocean

HIGHLIGHTS: Called Old Town by the merchants, and Lower State by most locals, the section of State Street from Ortega to the ocean is lined with one-of-a-kind shops, eateries and a thriving local club scene. A prominent merchant's sign refers to the area as a "zesty mix of ethnic restaurants, hotels, offices and enticing specialty shops."

Oceanward of the freeway, lower Lower State has a marine emphasis—surf and swimwear shops, seafood restaurants. Just off lower, Lower State are two not-to-be missed Santa Barbara sights: the Southern Pacific train station and the Moreton Bay Fig Tree.

DISTANCE: A mile from Ortega Street to Stearns Wharf.

TRANSPORTATION: Downtown/Waterfront Shuttle. By auto: Park in the Ortega Street parking garage located between State Street and Anacapa Street.

A QUICK look at lower State Street reveals that the area shows much promise, but it's obviously struggling. It's been a somewhat seedy neighborhood, complete with liquor stores, cheap hotels and even an adult bookstore. The street has been renovated with elimination of street parking, the addition of wrought-iron lamps, tiled planters and brick-like sidewalks. A decade-long redevelopment effort and the completion of the crosstown freeway guarantees that this section of State Street will continue to change considerably.

Santa Barbara has long had the dubious distinction among California cities of being the last to remove traffic lights from its section of U.S. Highway 101. Removal of the lights meant construction of the crosstown freeway. One of these lights was at State Street.

With the new, traffic light-less highway, State Street was routed under the freeway and an underpass now links State Street's beach area with the downtown section.

State Street ends (or begins, if your prefer) at Stearns Wharf, at one time Santa Barbara's major "port of entry." In tandem with the wharf, State Street grew to become the community's main thoroughfare for commercial trade. Hotels were built to serve the shipping trade, and with the dawn of the Automobile Age, several dealerships were established. Most of these businesses have moved to other locations, but the distinctive buildings remain.

THE WALK: Begin at the corner of State and Ortega, where buildings constructed nearly a century apart stand across the street from one another: Paseo Nuevo (circa 1990) on one side of the street, the Fithian Building (circa 1895) on the other. Joel Remington Fithian, civic mover and shaker, owner and director of the Santa Barbara Country Club, ordered the construction of this distinct structure, known as the Lower Clock Building. Before the 1925 earthquake, the Fithian Building was a 3½-story building, but its clock tower and top floor were severely damaged during the temblor and removed. Today, the building houses a popular watering hole and restaurant, and on its upper floor, a number of small businesses.

Locally grown produce was sold at 600 State Street at Rossi's Fruit Market, which opened for business in 1883. On Tuesday evenings from 4 P.M. to 7:30 P.M., the Certified Farmer's Market sets up on the 500 block, offering a tempting selection of healthful produce.

Continue down State, exploring the eclectic selection of specialty shops, and depending on the time of day, don't miss two Santa Barbara institutions, both usually packed with hungry locals and hopeful visitors. For breakfast, it's Esau's (403 State) for the best pancakes in town, and for lunch and dinner, make way for Joe's Cafe (536 State). Check out the Moorish-looking building with the tower and the pedestrian arcade at 318 State near the freeway.

Continue on State Street underneath Highway 101; you might want to stop first at one of the most popular coffee spots in town, the Santa Barbara Roasting Company, in the area called Sevilla Square by local merchants.

Bear right to the landmark Southern Pacific Railroad Depot, one of the last Mission Revival-style stations in California. As one turn-of-the-century railroad architect put it: "Give me neither Romanesque nor Gothic; much less Italian Renaissance and least of all English Colonial. This is California, give me Mission!"

After admiring the station, which has been in active service since 1905, walk to Chapala Street and turn right to view another city landmark, the giant Moreton Bay fig tree. It has grown from a seedling planted in 1877 to its present size of over 70 feet tall with a 10-foot diameter trunk. It was once a major attraction, second only to the Mission, but in recent years has become headquarters for Santa Barbara's homeless population, and now attracts fewer visitors.

Return to State Street. The fashion-conscious will note factory outlets: the Big Dogs Sierra West outlet at State and Yanonali and The Territory Ahead on Mason just east of State. On lower Lower State near the handsome, arcaded Californian Hotel, Allen and Malcolm Lockheed built their F-1 passenger airplane during the years 1916-21 before moving their business to Burbank.

Near the beach are surf and surfwear shops, cycle rental establishments and fish restaurants—everything you'd expect from a beach town. Walk back the way you came, return by the shuttle bus, or join one of the beachfront walks detailed in this guide.

9. Only on Sunday

HIGHLIGHTS: On Sundays in Santa Barbara, sights unseen the rest of the week are suddenly open to public view. Cabrillo Boulevard is transformed into a coloful art and craft show, and two historic houses and a carriage museum are unlocked and on view. It's a lot to take in for one day, but a little planning ahead can provide a unique adventure.

DISTANCE: The Cabrillo Art and Craft Show extends one-half mile along Cabrillo Boulevard from Stearns Wharf. So figure a mile round trip. Add another mile round trip to walk to the historic Fernald House, Trussell-Winchester Adobe and Old Spanish Days Carriage House.

INSIDER'S TIPS: When we say only on Sunday, we mean only on Sunday. You may want to linger, but realize that the historic houses and museum are only open once a week, for the same two hours. Plan your time carefully because there's a lot to see at each site. Admission to all three attractions is free, but donations to defray operating expenses are welcome.

TRANSPORTATION: Downtown/Waterfront Shuttle to Stearns Wharf.

By auto: The Cabrillo Boulevard exit from Highway 101 brings you to the art walk, and to Stearns Wharf. By midday, nearby parking might be difficult to find.

The Fernald House Trussell-Winchester Adobe and Old Spanish Days Carriage House are open Sunday afternoons, 2-4 only. The Cabrillo Craft Show hours are 10 A.M. to dark, rain or shine.

The Carriage Museum is located at 129 Castillo Street, in Pershing Park; the historic houses at 412 and 414 West Montecito Street.

STARTING at Stearns Wharf, and extending eastward for about a half-mile along palm-lined Chase Palm Park, is one of Santa Barbara's must-see attractions. Every Sunday, Cabrillo Boulevard is transformed into a colorful bazaar featuring the work of the most talented local artists and artisans. Hand-crafted clothing, jewelry and leather goods, pottery and ceramics, paintings and baskets, wind chimes and whimsical items that defy categorization are for sale; many of the artists are on hand to discuss their work with you.

When you've seen all the arts and crafts you can handle (or when you've run out of money paying for the ones you want to take home with you), return to Stearns Wharf and continue west on Cabrillo Street to Castillo Street, site of Pershing Park. Notice the graceful band shell, and head for the northwest end of the park to reach the Carriage Museum, which is located near the baseball fields.

If old-time carriages, horse-drawn carts and stagecoaches interest you, the Old Spanish Days Carriage Museum is the place for you. The museum maintains the largest collection of restored carriages in the West. The 75 coaches, wagons, carriages and other wheeled conveyances on display here range from a colorful seventeenth-century Sicilian wine cart to a somber nineteenth-century hearse. Plenty of Wild-West wagons and stagecoaches are also part of this extensive exhibit.

Every summer, several of the most elegant carriages transport public officials and civic leaders along the route of the Old Spanish Days Fiesta parade.

After you've finished browsing through the museum, return to Castillo Street and head north to Montecito Street (a busy intersection with traffic signals). Take a left turn on Montecito Street, and walk a half-block to the landmark site marked by a white picket fence and a large marker.

From outside appearances, the Trussell-Winchester Adobe looks more like it belongs in Cape Cod than in Santa Barbara. Once you get inside, however, the thick walls and low ranch style reveal its adobe construction.

The house was built in 1854 by Captain Horatio Gates Trussell, a seaman from Maine. Timbers salvaged from the Winfield Scott, a side-wheeler ship wrecked off Anacapa Island, form the basic foundation of the house, and locally produced adobe bricks complete it. The captain's sea chest and music box are on display, as well as personal effects belonging to the Winchester family, who later purchased the house.

Behind the captain's house is Fernald House. Built in 1862, this fourteen-room Victorian mansion reflects the life of Judge Fernald and his family. The elegant redwood staircase, stained-glass window above the front door, and a large number of family treasures are all highlights of this interesting house. The multi-gabled house, complete with front porch and sunroom, was moved to its present site from its original location on Santa Barbara Street, a couple of miles away.

Both the Trussell-Winchester Adobe and the Fernald House have been designated California Historical Landmarks. Docents from the Santa Barbara Historical Society lead informative half-hour tours of each house on Sunday afternoons only.

Return the same way, or consult Walk #15 for some engaging alternatives.

10. Santa Barbara Cemetery

HIGHLIGHTS: You'll view some notable frescoes, see a classic building designed by Santa Barbara's best-known architect, and stroll the quiet grounds that have served as the community's final resting place for more than a century. Don't expect grandiose Forest Lawn-like attractions, but there's a wonderful chapel here designed by famed architect George Washington Smith.

DISTANCE: A visit to the chapel and viewpoint in the military section is quite a short walk. If you walk around the grounds, it's about a mile walk.

INSIDER'S TIPS: Some think cemeteries are peaceful places that provide a glimpse into the culture, values and people of a place. Others find them depressing, even morbid. If you fall into the latter category, skip this walk. But if you fall into the former, come along with us.

TRANSPORTATION: The Santa Barbara Cemetery is located at the east end of Cabrillo Boulevard, where it meets Channel Drive (the road that goes up to the Biltmore). The MTD drops you off on the right, just past the cemetery entrance.

If you're arriving by car, exit Highway 101 on Cabrillo Boulevard (a left-lane offramp). Turn oceanward on Cabrillo and be prepared to make an awkward left turn (be very careful) on Channel Drive. Look sharply right for the drive leading to the Cemetery.

Park near the Sanctuary of Life Eternal.

WALK past the "Visitors Welcome" sign into the chapel, a fine place for contemplation before you begin your walk around the grounds. Designed in 1926 by architect George Washington Smith, the graceful Romanesque/Gothic chapel has long been regarded as one of his masterpieces.

The founding director of the Santa Barbara Museum of Art, Donald Bear, wrote: "The simple, intimate, yet somehow noble

beauty of the building is a genuine tribute to the landscape. Inside the chapel this very beauty is further sustained by the Martinez murals."

The "Martinez murals" are the frescoes applied to the interior walls by famed Mexican painter Alfredo Ramos Martinez. After Smith's death in 1930, his widow commissioned Martinez to paint the frescoes. The striking artwork is a must-see for every art enthusiast.

Linger awhile to absorb the impact of the fine artwork with its garlands of flowers, handmaidens, monks and nuns moving toward the startlingly dominant figure of the resurrected Christ. Then wander through the chapel, noting the markers of several notable Santa Barbarans. Architects George Washington Smith and Lutah Maria Riggs are both interred in the chapel wall. Downstairs from the chapel is a Gothic-style columbarium worth a look, and across the way is the Mausoleum in the Pines.

Cemeteries always seem to inspire stories and Santa Barbara's is no exception. Aldous Huxley is said to be buried in an unmarked grave somewhere on the property. And local lore has it that several barons, princes, dukes and counts—who never even visited Santa Barbara— are buried here because it's known as one of the most beautiful cemeteries in the world.

Uphill from the chapel is the cemetery's military section, marked with an American flag and a large cannon. Stroll through and you'll note that veterans from every war since the Civil War are buried here. From this hillock is a wonderful view—from the Santa Ynez Mountains to the Riviera and on to the ocean. It's nice to think that the permanent residents are enjoying the spot. At least their visitors do.

Head uphill and rightward toward the family mausoleum area. You'll see several tombs—in styles representing everything from a classic Greek temple to an Egyptian pyramid. Read some of the headstones and markers; they tell many stories. A brotherhood of young motorcyclists laid to rest in one section, infant and young children in another. Grouped in other sections are immigrants—Italian, Greek, Mexican, Chinese, Japanese, English.

At the southwest end of the cemetery, peer over the fence for a view of the magnificent Clark mansion. The 22-acre estate, "Bellos-guardo" (beautiful lookout) was once the summer home of turn-of-the-century U.S. Senator William A. Clark. Beyond the estate is a lovely view of the harbor.

Continue walking in a counter-clockwise circuit of the cemetery. On the oceanward side of the drive, on the bluffs, are buried many of Santa Barbara's one-time civic leaders including Pearl Chase, Thomas More Storke, the Castagnola brothers. The sharp-eyed will spot the ornate wrought-iron cross marking the graves of architects Mary and James Osborne Craig. Continuing east, then looping back toward the chapel, notice the oldest headstones, dating back to the nineteenth century.

11. Montecito

HIGHLIGHTS: Montecito has always been one of Santa Barbara's most fashionable neighborhoods. This easy walk takes you from a historic hotel, through a lovely shopping area to Butterfly Beach, the Biltmore and more.
DISTANCE: 1½ miles round trip.
TRANSPORTATION: The MTD along the waterfront takes you to Coast Village Road and Olive Mill Road in Montecito. By auto, exit Highway 101 at Olive Mill Road. Park on or near Coast Village Drive. This walk begins in front of the Montecito Inn, 1295 Coast Village Road.

THE Franciscan padres once considered Montecito for the site of their Mission, but decided against it because of the abundance of grizzly bears and wolves in the area. The lovely spot (Montecito is Spanish for "small forest") became a rich agricultural area in the nineteenth century, and a playground/hideaway for the rich and famous ever since. Although there are a few modest Montecito dwellings, in some neighborhoods the term "Montecito mansion" is redundant; the area is noted for its stately homes, quiet, tree-lined streets and decidedly affluent ambience.

Old-time movie stars frequented the Mediterranean-style hotel first owned by Hollywood's own Charlie Chaplin and "Fatty" Arbuckle. Recently renovated, the hotel still maintains its original style and charm.

THE WALK: Head down the sidewalk past Montecito Grill, a favorite local jazz club, and pass—on both sides of the street—several excellent restaurants, interesting shops and quite an assortment of real estate offices. Stop for a bite, browse awhile and speculate—if your pocketbook allows. Enjoy the feeling and sophisticated elegance of the area, sometimes called the Rodeo Drive of Santa Barbara.

At Butterfly Lane, turn left and descend a stairwell into the pedestrian tunnel that takes you under the freeway. Stroll the estate-lined street to its end and head for the coastal accessway at Butterfly Beach.

Continue east along the beachfront road, Channel Drive, to Biltmore Beach and its Coral Casino, site of numerous glittering social events. The Coral Casino, with a restaurant and Olympic-size swimming pool is a private beach club.

Admire the Biltmore, which has set the Santa Barbara standard for elegance since it opened in 1927. The gracious architecture and lovely grounds are something to behold.

Stay with Channel Drive as it turns inland and becomes Olive Mill Road, leading you over the freeway to Coast Village Road and your starting point.

12. University of California at Santa Barbara

HIGHLIGHTS: UCSB is the third-largest UC campus. Although the university has a "party school" reputation, it's also known for excellent academic programs. While the campus architecture is, to say the least, uninspired, the stunning coastal location makes up for the dull buildings. And you have to see Isla Vista, with its remarkably high student population.

DISTANCE: A mile round trip.

TRANSPORTATION: The isolated campus is actually located in Isla Vista, 10 miles from downtown Santa Barbara. The Santa Barbara/UCSB Express MTD bus takes you from the Transit Center to North Hall. Several other MTD routes also stop at North Hall.

If you're arriving by car, take Highway 101 to Goleta, veering south on Clarence Ward Memorial Boulevard (217) and following the signs to UCSB. At the entry kiosk on weekdays, you'll pay a parking fee and receive a campus map and directions. There's convenient parking in a lot off University Road opposite North Hall.

THE University of California at Santa Barbara was thrust into the national spotlight during the sixties when war protestors burned the Isla Vista Bank of America. But today, that same building houses a disco, and everything is comparatively peaceful and very quiet for a college community. Adjacent to campus are high-rise student housing buildings, fraternity rows and sorority houses. Bike paths crisscross the campus, indeed the entire Isla Vista area, and they receive heavy use. When walking through the area, be sure to use caution when crossing bike paths.

THE WALK: To explore the UCSB campus, start at Cheadle Hall, the university's administration building, which includes Admissions, Graduate Division, and the chancellor's office.

Head toward Campbell Hall, where films, lectures, dance, musical and theatrical performances are often featured.

Take the diagonal pathway and head for the back entrance of the library, which houses 1.75 million volumes. Inside the library, take the elevator up to the eighth floor for a wonderful view of the area. From the north windows, get a great view of the rugged Santa Ynez mountains, with the airport on the right.

From the east windows, take in the view of Goleta Pier, and a surprising amount of open space. From this vantage point, obvious that Santa Barbara is some 10 miles down-coast from Isla Vista.

From the south windows, view dormitory housing across the way, the ocean and Channel Islands beyond. There are several favorite surfing, skindiving, snorkeling and sunworshipping beach spots nearby, including Campus Point, Depression and Sands.

Return to the first floor, and leave the library from the front door, heading west toward 175-foot Storke Tower, tallest structure in Santa Barbara County. The bell tower's observation deck is occasionally open. The bells chime at 10 minutes to the hour (class dismissed!) and on the hour (time for class to begin). The university's communication center is located at the base of the tower; the newspaper, yearbook and programs for public radio station KCSB-FM are produced here.

Adjacent to the tower is Storke Plaza, the usually bustling main quad area. Head toward University Center, called UCen by students. Inside are commercial services including a travel agency, post office, copy center and typing service, along with three restaurants, the bookstore, a grocery store and entertainment room. The activities board just inside the hallway always offers plenty to do.

Head for the art museum which features exhibitions year-round, then stroll into Isla Vista, about five minutes away. It's a land of 99-cent burgers and monster beers, falafel and pot stickers, reflecting the international tastes of 16,000 students who attend one of California's most desirable campuses.

Short Walks and Special Stops

Brinkerhoff Avenue

Located two blocks west of the 500 block of State Street, between Cota and Haley streets, is a landmark district of Victorian homes, many of which have been converted into antique shops and galleries. Shop for fine furniture, handmade linens, crystal and gift items.

The avenue named for Dr. Samuel Brinkerhoff, first physician to practice in Santa Barbara, is lined with homes (some private residences, some used as shops) designed in a mixture of turn-of-the-century styles, including Queen Anne, Colonial Revival and Italianate. Together with a few Mission Revival structures on Chapala and Cota, they form the Brinkerhoff Avenue Landmark District, established in 1982.

Farmer's Certified Market

Twice a week, shop for fresh produce, healthy plants, colorful flowers and more, straight from the farmer to you. On Saturday morning at the corner of Cota and Santa Barbara streets, two blocks east of State Street, from 8:30 A.M. to 12:00 noon; on Tuesday evening at the 500 block of State Street from 4 P.M. to 7:30 P.M. Bring a shopping bag, basket or canvas sack to carry your treats, and save the planet, too.

Santa Barbara Firescapes Demonstration Garden

Stroll through this tiny pocket park and get an education at the same time. Located across the street from Fire Station #7 at 2411 Stanwood Drive (at the corner of Stanwood and Sycamore Canyon Road). Designed by Santa Barbara landscape architect Owen Dell following the devastating Sycamore Canyon Fire in 1977, the four-zone system explained and demonstrated here could help save your home in the event of wildfire. An added bonus: Most of the plants in this garden are hardy, drought-tolerant natives.

Haley Street

You would never see this street recommended by a travel brochure. It's a grittier Santa Barbara than you expect; and you wouldn't want to head down there after sunset—too many unsavory characters engaged in questionable activities. But on a Saturday afternoon, it's a great place to enjoy authentic Mexican cuisine, get a close-up glimpse of one of Santa Barbara's ethnic neighborhoods, and stop in a few notable shops.

Between State and Milpas streets, it's a light-industrial area, comparable to Pico and Sepulveda in West Los Angeles. Community-supported residence hotels, auto repair and body shops dot the street, along with small businesses dealing with tools, tiles, glass and plumbing supplies. Not to be missed are two special attractions: a tortilla factory and a ceramics studio.

The Santa Barbara Ceramic Design Studio Outlet is located in the 400 block of East Haley. You've seen their handcrafted frames, clocks, tiles and address plaques in upscale shops and boutiques. This is the place where you can purchase them at special (low) prices. Friendly folks and a good selection make this a favorite place to buy nice gifts—for loved ones and for yourself.

La Tolteca, located at 614 East Haley, has been a Santa Barbara institution since 1952. The restaurant features tasty Mexican food, and also distributes tortillas to supermarkets, groceries and eateries throughout the Central Coast. In a large room adjacent to the food service is an amazing tortilla machine that churns out something like 14,000 dozen tortillas a day!

You'll soon reach Milpas Street. At the corner of Haley and Milpas, in a brick building, is Santa Barbara's first Thai restaurant; there's another one a few blocks south. Despite the proliferation of ethnic eateries—within a few blocks are Italian, Chinese, New Mexican, Greek and all-American sandwich shop—Milpas is the main street through Santa Barbara's Hispanic neighborhood. It's the center of the community, a place where you'll hear more Spanish than English. The Milpas area is referred to by a number of names—"the barrio," "lower east side," or even "Baja Riviera." It is the home of thousands of Santa Barbarans, some of whom have roots here going back a hundred years.

TRANSPORTATION: The Downtown/Waterfront Shuttle takes you down State Street to Haley, where this walk begins. If you walk the length of Haley to Milpas, you can bus back to State Street. The MTD bus travels up Milpas to State and Anapamu, or back to the transit center.

Montecito Village

It's the ultimate picnic destination, a wonderful shopping excursion, and a delightful stroll down a country lane lined with storybook cottages. All this in less than a mile's walk.

Start at Montecito's Plaza del Sol, at the corner of San Ysidro and East Valley roads. Walk facing traffic just two blocks; there's a good-sized shoulder, but be careful. Walk east on East Valley to the second street on the left, Periwinkle Lane. Turn onto the graded dirt lane, and stroll through a fragrant wonderland of eucalyptus and oak trees, morning glory vines, and lovely gingerbread houses. This fairytale neighborhood was built in the '40s by architect Harriet Moody.

Follow Periwinkle Lane as it curves around to Hodges, turn left, then right on East Valley Road, and return to your starting point. Explore the shops here and at Coast Village across the street, dine at the popular Italian eateries Piatti or Pane e Vino Trattoria (or make reservations for another time).

For an unforgettable treat, don't miss Pierre LaFond and Company, an upscale gourmet shop/department store like no other. Here you may rent a picnic basket complete with checked tablecloth and wine glasses, and order deluxe treats for a sumptuous picnic. Then head south down San Ysidro a couple of blocks to Manning Park. Spread out your luncheon and savor the day.

TRANSPORTATION: The MTD to East Valley and San Ysidro. By auto: Highway 101 to San Ysidro Road, north at exit to the intersection with East Valley Road. Park at the shopping center.

COAST

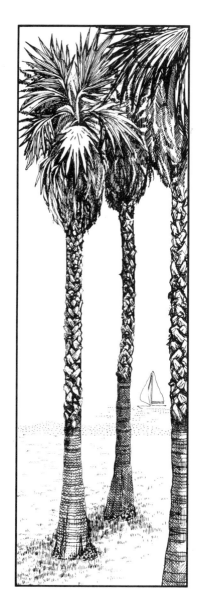

Coast

FROM Carpinteria west, the Santa Barbara County shoreline extends to Point Conception, one sandy and mellow beach after another. The coastline's southern exposure results in clearer water, smoother sand and warmer sun than other California communities. Or so the locals like to boast, anyway. The beach is lined by a narrow coastal terrace that seems to protect it from residences, traffic, the hustle and bustle of the modern world.

Enhanced by the Mediterranean climate, Santa Barbara's beaches have long been world renowned for their beauty and as a place to play. Sailing, surfing and sunbathing are popular shoreline activities.

The Santa Barbara coast has an ecological significance as well. Marine life is abundant and a large percentage of the state's fish and shellfish catch comes from the Santa Barbara Channel.

Many Santa Barbarans—and conservationists around the country—are concerned about the region's delicate ecology and fragile beauty. Oil drilling in the Santa Barbara Channel is particularly worrisome. The devastation brought by a 1969 oil spill is never far from the the citizenry's mind. Debates about tanker traffic, pipelines, processing plants and lease sales continue to this day.

For thousands of years before Europeans arrived, Chumash Indians, the most ocean-oriented of California's native peoples, lived along Santa Barbara's shores. They fished off the coast in dugout canoes, hunted in the nearby mountains. From the days of the missionaries and Spanish occupation through most of the nineteenth century, the coastline remained mostly undeveloped.

New England trading ships anchored offshore to take on a cargo of cowhides from local ranchers, but Santa Barbara was anything but a thriving seaport. Santa Barbara's "lighthouse" was a lantern hung at the top of a tree known as "Sailors' Sycamore."

Lack of a safe port hindered Santa Barbara's development. The bay was merely a lovely curve in the coast, offering a landing place but no protection from the dreaded southeasters. Until John P. Stearns built his wharf in 1872, landing in Santa Barbara meant braving the breakers with small surf boats; passengers often got a refreshing salt water dip before arriving on shore.

With safe steamer landings, visitors—ranging from wealthy residents of colder climates looking for a place to winter, to invalids (as they called them in Victorian times) seeking to restore their health—flocked to Santa Barbara. The "Sanitarium of the Pacific" got a big boost from Charles Nordhoff's 1872 bestseller *California For Travelers and Settlers,* which raved about Santa Barbara's charms and promoted it as a health resort.

Health-seekers and tourists gave Santa Barbara an international reputation, though world-class facilities to handle the visitors lagged far behind. Not until the Potter Hotel opened in 1902 was there a large oceanfront hotel. Fears of rampaging waves from Pacific storms meant the Arlington Hotel and others were built well inland.

For most of the twentieth century, the coastline has been the subject of much debate among Santa Barbarans, between those who wanted to exploit the shore's full revenue potential as a resort, and those who wanted to conserve the coast's natural beauty. Many Santa Barbarans wanted to ensure that only a wealthy tourist class came to Santa Barbara, while others welcomed out-of-town developers who would build facilities to attract the middle class in great numbers. Both the Chamber of Commerce and wealthy philanthropists helped purchase oceanfront land and thwart tawdry developments and "undesirable amusement."

It was the automobile and a changing economy that brought

changes to the waterfront. Wealthy part-time residents were not as influential as middle class auto tourists on vacation. After World War II came a motel boom that serviced these visitors.

Whether it's a large hotel project such as the Red Lion or the design of a small fountain, Santa Barbarans are likely to debate this issue of aesthetics versus economics, open space versus commercial building well into the next century.

Awaiting the walker are miles of pleasant sand beach with the ocean and islands on one side and the mountains on the other. Besides the picture-postcard beaches near Santa Barbara, the county has another coast, a wild coast. This is the north coast near Point Conception, characterized by rolling hills, marshlands and precipitous bluffs. A walk along land's end here can be an unforgettable adventure.

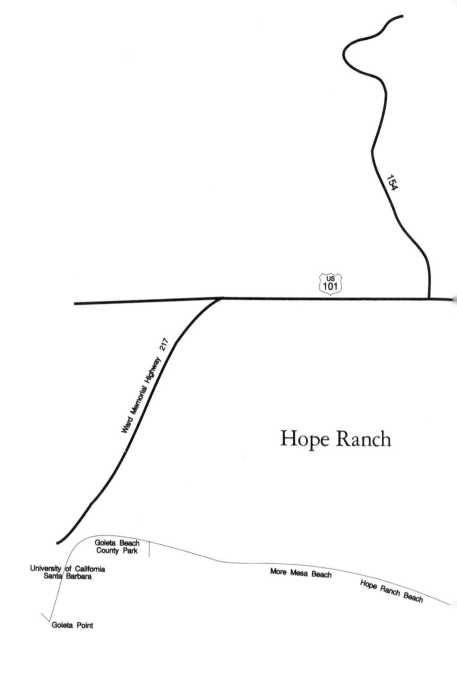

154

US
101

Ward Memorial Highway 217

Hope Ranch

Goleta Beach
County Park

University of California
Santa Barbara

More Mesa Beach

Hope Ranch Beach

Goleta Point

Pacific Ocean

Santa Barbara
Coast

Santa Barbara

US 101

Andrea Clark
Bird Refuge

State Visitors Center

Santa Barbara
Zoological Gardens

East Beach

Castillo

Chase Palm Park

Sea Center and
Nature Conservancy

West Beach

Los Baños
Del Mar

Stearns Wharf

225 Las Positas

Santa Barbara Harbor

Cliff Drive 225

Cabrillo

Leadbetter Beach

Castillo

Shoreline Park

One Thousand
Steps

▲
Lighthouse

Arroyo Burro Beach
County Park

Pacific Ocean

13. Stearns Wharf

HIGHLIGHTS: Fun, fish and great sunset views from the longest wharf between Los Angeles and San Francisco.
DISTANCE: Not far.
INSIDER'S TIPS: Don't overlook the Sea Center on the "dog leg" part of the wharf.
TRANSPORTATION: Downtown/Waterfront Shuttle
    (Nature Conservancy exhibits are open weekdays noon to 4 P.M. and weekends 11 A.M. to 5 P.M. Admission is free. Sea Center hours: 10 A.M. to 5 P.M., outside touch tank open noon to 4, closed on Monday; admission is $2 adults; $1.50 seniors; $1 ages 3-17.

BEFORE John Peck Stearns built his wharf in 1872, Santa Barbara, like so many California coastal towns, was isolated from the rest of the world. Only San Diego and San Francisco were blessed with natural harbors; other cities, big and small, needed some ingenuity to construct landing facilities.

Stearns provided the solution for Santa Barbara. With financial help from Colonel W.W. Hollister, the peg-legged lumber yard owner built a long wharf—the longest, in fact, between Los Angeles and San Francisco. Passenger steamships could tie up at the 1,500-foot wharf, which greatly aided Santa Barbara's emergence as a health and vacation resort. Cargo ships unloaded the lumber and building materials so necessary for the city's Victorian-era building boom.

Steamships continued bringing thousands of visitors to Santa Barbara well into the twentieth century, but as alternate means of transportation developed, the wharf's commercial importance began to decline. At the turn of the century, when the coastal rail line was finally completed, thus linking Santa Barbara to Los Angeles and San

Francisco, many visitors began arriving by train. By the 1920s, a significant number of visitors arrived by auto.

With more and more visitors, the wharf itself became a tourist attraction. The old yacht club building was converted to the Harbor Restaurant in 1941 and its reputation soon spread far and wide.

During World War II, the military took over Stearns Wharf and was less-than-enthusiastic about its maintenance. Film star Jimmy Cagney and his brothers bought the wharf in 1945. The Cagneys' ambitious plans for reconstruction never materialized when they realized a small fortune in repairs was necessary.

Mario and George Castagnola purchased the wharf in 1955 and restored it. The Moby Dick Restaurant, gift shops, a bait-and-tackle shop and the Harbor Restaurant were popular with visitors during the 1950s and '60s. All of these structures were destroyed by fire in 1973.

The city took over the wharf's operation, and after several years of political and economic discussions, rebuilt it into the popular attraction it is today.

For strolling and shopping, fishing and sunset-watching, Stearns Wharf is the place to go. It's not uncommon for the walker to overhear a half-dozen languages on the wharf; like the Mission, it attracts visitors from around the world.

Parking is limited and the city encourages visitors to walk the wharf. It's a walk just about everyone can—and should—do. Advice to heed comes in the form of two whimsical international signs posted at the foot of the wharf that read: "No high-heel shoes" and "No bare feet."

THE WALK: At the wharf entrance is the Dolphin fountain created by local artist Bud Bottoms. Copies of this fountain have been presented to Santa Barbara's sister cities.

If you read every plaque and interpretive panel on the wharf, you'd get quite an oceanography lesson. "Shifting Sands," "What Causes Tides?" and many more panels tell the story of Santa Barbara's harbor, islands, sea life and explorers.

The wharf offers great views of East Beach and Chase Palm Park, West Beach and the harbor. Don't forget to look behind you at the Riviera and the Santa Ynez Mountains. This view can also be enjoyed from the Harbor Restaurant and the outside deck of its bar.

Continue walking toward two more eateries, the Moby Dick Restaurant and the Santa Barbara Shellfish Company. On Stearns Wharf, you can have a fish dinner, get a shrimp cocktail to go, or cast a line and catch a fish of your own, as you'll notice many Santa Barbarans doing.

On the west side of the wharf are several gift shops selling everything from shark jerky to ice cream, as well as locally produced arts and crafts. Mixed in with the shops are a palm reader and a wine-tasting room.

Out on the "dog leg" of the wharf is the Nature Conservancy Visitor Center. Exhibits highlighting the Conservancy's California preserves, as well as the organization's administrative offices are found here.

Also on the dog leg is the Sea Center, with terrific exhibits of the marine life of Channel Islands National Park. This joint project with the Santa Barbara Museum of Natural History and the Channel Islands Marine Sanctuary features aquariums, an art gallery, a topographical map of Channel Islands and a replica of a California gray whale.

14. East Beach and Beyond

HIGHLIGHTS: Chase Palm Park, Cabrillo Pavillion, zoo, bird sanctuary and a beach that's been popular with locals and visitors for more than a century.
DISTANCE: Chase Palm Park is a mile long. Add another mile if you continue to the bird sanctuary.
INSIDER'S TIPS: Local artists display their work along the Cabrillo Boulevard side of Chase Palm Park every Sunday. For a healthy picnic, get supplies at Tri-County Produce, located one block up Milpas from the beach. Zoo hours 10 A.M. to 5 P.M. daily; 9 A.M. to 6 P.M. in summer. Admission: Adults $4; seniors and children 2-12 $2; under 2 free.
TRANSPORTATION: This walk begins at Stearns Wharf at the foot of State Street. The Downtown/Waterfront Shuttle gets you there.

IT'S the postcard view of Santa Barbara: Sandy beach, Chase Palm Park, white walls and red roofs, the Riviera and the Santa Ynez Mountains.

East Beach is the classic Southern California beach—long, sandy and rarely crowded. It's the place to play—beach volleyball, boogie boarding, sand sculpture contests—and the place to relax, with ample square footage of sand for the discriminating sunbather.

By the 1870s, wealthy health-seekers were flocking to Santa Barbara. And East Beach is where they flocked. Horse-drawn streetcars (electrified in 1896) traveled the length of East Beach, bringing bathers from the bathhouses to the beach.

Historians credit architect Peter Barber with the idea for a palm-lined shoreline drive along East Beach. Barber got his idea after visiting tree-lined avenues in Europe. As mayor of Santa Barbara in 1891, he helped win voter approval for the bond measure that beautified the beach area and made Cabrillo Boulevard (then East Beach Boulevard) the scenic drive it is today.

Another visionary, perhaps the quintessential Santa Barbara citizen of her era, Pearl Chase, also crusaded to preserve the coastline. Chase and her brother Harold were honored when the city renamed Palm Park, created in 1931, Chase Palm Park.

The walker has three ways to explore East Beach: the sidewalk along Cabrillo Boulevard (the best option on Sundays when the weekly art sale takes place), along the beach itself, or our favorite, a stroll through Chase Palm Park. The park is a bit more than a mile long. Near its east end is Cabrillo Pavillion, where you can break for refreshments, see an art show or rent a boogie board.

THE WALK: Your path through the *Washingtonia robusta* palms soon takes you over the mouth of Mission Creek.

At the foot of Santa Barbara Street, you'll find a plaque commemorating Pearl and Harold Chase for their civic and conservation efforts. At the corner of Santa Barbara Street and Cabrillo Boulevard is the Chamber of Commerce Visitor Center, one of the tiniest buildings in town. Built in 1911, and located around the corner on State Street, the sandstone structure formerly housed a fish market and restaurant. Pick up maps, brochures, event calendars, and plenty of additional visitor information here. (Open 9 A.M. to 5 P.M. Monday through Saturday; 10 A.M. to 4 P.M. on Sunday.)

After a bit more meandering through the palms you'll see Fess Parker's Red Lion Resort on the north side of Cabrillo Boulevard. The large round building is a re-creation of a Southern Pacific Railroad Roundhouse, which was used to handle steam locomotives from 1926 to 1961. After the 1925 earthquake damaged an earlier roundhouse, it was Pearl Chase who showed Southern Pacific officials a favorite postcard of a bullring in Seville and convinced them to build this most utilitarian of structures in the Spanish motif. The roundhouse was razed in 1982 and the "roundhouse" you see today is part of the hotel and convention center.

The Red Lion Hotel itself, successfully pushed through many layers of government regulation by actor-turned-developer Fess Parker (Davy Crockett, Daniel Boone), was a controversial project in the mid-eighties, because of its size and scale. The Mission Revival buildings take the historic Spanish motif and offer beach and mountain views. You can't miss the Chromatic Gate, the geometric rainbow situated on the corner.

Another Santa Barbara luxury hotel in Spanish style, located a little farther along Cabrillo Boulevard, is the Santa Barbara Radisson Hotel. Formerly the Vista Mar Monte, the hotel was completed in 1930 at a then-astronomical cost of $5 million, attracted film industry executives and Hollywood stars in the 1930s, and is still popular with celebrities today. During President Ronald Reagan's two terms in office, 1981-89, when Santa Barbara was the Western White House, the national press corps headquartered in the then-Sheraton.

SIDETRIP: Just beyond the Radisson, turn left at Ninos Drive and walk a block along Dwight Murphy ball field to the Santa Barbara Zoological Gardens. Here you'll find a zoo with more than 500 animals and 50 exhibits atop a knoll overlooking East Beach. With a nature theater, children's train and children's petting zoo, this is a great place to take the kids.

At the end of Palm Park, skirt the small parking lot and proceed to Cabrillo Pavillion, or Cabrillo Arts Center, as it's sometimes called. A plaque honors philanthropist David Gray, who donated the building to the people of Santa Barbara.

The Cabrillo Boulevard entrance leads to an art gallery with monthly exhibits of local artists. On the beach side is East Beach Café, as well as a public bathhouse with changing rooms, lockers and a weight room. The bathhouse rents boogie boards, sand chairs, umbrellas and volleyballs and sells all sorts of sun care products.

Beyond Cabrillo Pavillion is another half-mile of East Beach with a turfed picnic area and very popular beach volleyball courts. Walk to the end of the picnic area and (carefully) cross Cabrillo Boulevard to Andree Clark Bird Refuge, where cormorants, egrets, herons and many species of ducks reside. Bird-watchers have sighted nearly 200 species in the 42-acre wildlife refuge.

The refuge was originally a tidal marsh which some Santa Barbarans figured would make an ideal harbor. The Clark family donated monies to excavate the marsh and create a freshwater lake, which was named in memory of the donor's daughter, Andree.

You can follow the grassy perimeter between the bike path and the lake shore about halfway around the lake. The refuge, which had fallen upon hard times during the 1980s, is currently being restored by the city. The path ends near a big bend in Cabrillo Boulevard.

Directly across the street from the end of the bike path is Las Aves, an office complex. Cross Los Patos Street and head into the courtyard area to view a colorful fountain entitled, "It's Raining."

Il pleut, say the French, *stuhuy,* say the Chumash, *ame-ga hutte imasu,* say the Japanese. Whatever the language, the whimsical fountain is a delight. Embedded with cracked pottery, cup handles, and bits of china; surely it's one-of-a-kind.

Head back to Cabrillo Boulevard, and carefully cross to the stone plaza with bench, fountain and watering trough. This City Landmark was donated in 1911 by a prominent physician. The fountain originally included drinking facilities for human, equine and canine visitors, but it's been dry for years.

Friendship Fountain

Las Aves Fountain

15. West Beach and Santa Barbara Harbor

HIGHLIGHTS: Santa Barbara's harbor and breakwater. Also Shoreline Park and some unique resort architecture.
DISTANCE: Stearns Wharf to harbor, breakwater, 1½ miles round trip. To Shoreline Park, 3 miles round trip.
INSIDER'S TIPS: Walking the breakwater on a stormy day is a great experience. During winter months, migrating California gray whales can be sighted from Shoreline Park.
TRANSPORTATION: Begin at Stearns Wharf at the foot of State Street. Take the MTD Downtown/Waterfront Shuttle.

EVER wonder where you could keep your 250-foot luxury yacht?

No? Well, neither have we, but in the mid-1920s yeast magnate Max C. Fleischmann had a quite a parking problem—no anchorage for his *Haida*. He donated $200,000 to Santa Santa Barbara to build a breakwater, if the city would match funds.

Unfortunately, city fathers and harbor boosters took Fleischmann up on his offer and ignored warnings of engineers who said a break-water at West Beach would interrupt ocean currents and sand flow to beaches downcoast. The harbor was built at West Beach and almost immediately, downcoast beaches, from nearby Biltmore Beach to as far away as Rincon in Ventura County, began to suffer sand deprivation.

Today, the harbor is the beautiful home to many pleasure craft and a small commercial fishing fleet. And Santa Barbara beaches are sandy and inviting. But this beauty and sand comes at a price: much dredging and expense is continually needed to keep the harbor mouth open, the beaches supplied with sand.

This walk explores West Beach and the marina, as well as Shoreline Park. An optional return route points out some of the Spanish Mission Revival-style architecture that drew—and still draws—visitors to Santa Barbara.

THE WALK: Saunter up-coast along the beach or on the sidewalk along Cabrillo Boulevard. Near the end of the beach, at the corner of Castillo and Cabrillo (an example of those similar-sounding Spanish street names that drive visitors mad!) is Los Baños del Mar, site of the municipal pool.

Head for the water now. You'll spot Sea Landing, a small dock that serves as headquarters for charter fishing boats and a boat-launching facility. Join the walkway that leads along the marina, where a diversity of pleasure craft are moored. The ocean beyond the breakwater might look tranquil; however, for the sailor, the rough seas and unpredictable weather of the Santa Barbara Channel can provide quite a challenge to seamanship.

At the breakwater, turn left and walk past the U.S. Naval Reserve building on your right.

Just past the Navy building, you'll find a seafood restaurant, yacht brokers, marine supply store, as well as an unloading dock for the fishing fleet. At day's end, you can often watch the fishermen unload their catch from the boats and onto trucks. About 90 percent of Southern California's abalone and shrimp come from the Channel.

Continue along the harborside walkway to a plaque commemorating Santa Barbara's commercial fishing fleet, and to a statue of a boy riding a seahorse donated by Santa Barbara's sister city of Puerto Vallarta. To the right is the Santa Barbara Yacht Club. Members get great sunset views from the club's twin wraparound decks. Nonmembers get their view from out on the breakwater.

Walk out onto the breakwater, which horseshoe-curves around to the east to protect the harbor. Along the harbor side of the breakwater are flags representing various Santa Barbara civic and community service groups. If it's a windy day, hold onto your hat! Sometimes when the wind whips the ocean, saltwater sprays over the sea wall and douses breakwater walkers. The breakwater can be an exciting walk when a storm is rising!

[92]

If you want to explore more of Santa Barbara's waterfront, return to the vicinity of the yacht club and follow Leadbetter Beach, or cut through the parking lot if you insist, toward Santa Barbara Point. Leadbetter Beach is largely a man-made creation; construction of the harbor caused a large amount of sand to be deposited here. Above you, across Cabrillo Boulevard, is Santa Barbara City College. A sidewalk leads you up to Shoreline Park, a grassy strip along La Mesa Bluff overlooking the Pacific.

Picnicking and whale-watching (in winter) are two popular park activities.

For a glimpse at Santa Barbara's beachfront architecture, past and present, return to the infamous Castillo/Cabrillo intersection, and walk back toward the wharf along the north (mountain) side of Cabrillo Boulevard.

A short distance away is palm-lined Ambassador Park, where a plaque commemorates Burton Mound, one of Santa Barbara's most significant archeological sites. Here stood the Chumash village of Syukhtun, "where two trails run," and a burial site. At one time, the 30-foot high, 600-foot by 500-foot mound, belonged to former fur trader Lewis Burton, who was elected Santa Barbara's first American mayor in 1850.

Milo M. Potter made a molehill out of a mound when he built his opulent Potter Hotel in 1902. The Mission Revival-style hotel featured a telephone in every room. It was completely destroyed by fire in 1921.

All mourned the Potter's passing except archeologists, who dug up many Chumash artifacts before all but this small park was subdivided. Only the double row of palm trees, which once lined the promenade leading to the entrance of the Potter Hotel remain.

Spanish Revival architecture fans will want to meander through the park to the pleasant side streets near Cabrillo Boulevard. Mixed in with the motels are small courts and residences that reflect both the best of this architecture and some absolutely kitschy knock-offs.

Before returning to Stearns Wharf, take a peek at Villa Rosa at 15 Chapala Street, a breathtaking example of Spanish Colonial Revival architecture. The former Belevedere Apartments, now a bed-and-breakfast, is a gem of a building.

16. One Thousand Steps

HIGHLIGHTS: A long stairwell, but nowhere near a thousand steps, leads to the beach just up-coast from Shoreline Park. A second stairwell descends from the park to the beach. This walk explores the beach below the tall bluffs of Santa Barbara's Mesa neighborhood and returns through the Wilcox Property, currently privately held and the only undeveloped coastal bluff property within the city limits.

DISTANCE: 2 miles one-way from One Thousand Steps to Arroyo Burro County Park.

TRANSPORTATION: MTD bus to Shoreline Drive and Santa Cruz Boulevard.

By auto: From Stearns Wharf at the foot of State Street, head west (up-coast) along Cabrillo Boulevard, which soon becomes Shoreline Drive and reaches Shoreline Park. Park in the lot near the somewhat camouflaged large wooden stairway. Or continue until you reach Santa Cruz Boulevard, which is not a boulevard at all, but a tiny residential street. Park along Shoreline Drive. Thousand Steps, if open, is accessible at the coastal end of Santa Cruz Boulevard.

INSIDER TIPS: Consult a tidetable. This beach is best, sometimes only possible, at low tide. There's bus service from this walk's destination, Arroyo Burro County Park, if you want to make this a one-way walk.

THE blufftop where you begin this walk is part of a marine terrace that includes Shoreline Park. Geologists call it a fault scarp that was created by movement along the Mesa Fault. Some earth scientists speculate that Santa Barbara's devastating 1925 earthquake was caused by movement along this fault.

Back of the beach is the hump of a land separating downtown from the sea called "The Mesa." It's a Spanish word meaning table. Japanese farmers settled in this area and established nurseries and flower farms. By the 1920s a Sunday drive out to the flower farms was a popular family outing.

Today the Mesa is a mellow middle-class neighborhood, whose residents enjoy the access they have to both beach and town.

The (only) two coastal access points from the Mesa are via Thousand Steps and Shoreline Park. Much to the frustration of coastal access activists and a thousand walkers, the city closed venerable Thousand Steps in 1992, citing high maintenance costs for the closure; its future is clouded. Check to see if the steps are accessible before you begin this walk.

THE WALK: Walk to the end of Santa Cruz Boulevard to the viewpoint. The Santa Barbara Lighthouse, located up-coast, was first lit in 1856 and was tended by Captain Albert Williams and his wife Julia for forty years. Destroyed by the great Santa Barbara earthquake of 1925, it was replaced by an automated light.

Descend the steps to the beach and enjoy the solitude that this sandy and cobble beach usually brings. About a mile's hike brings you to the Mesa Lane Stairs, the only coastal access point between One Thousand Steps and Arroyo Burro Beach County Park. Continue another mile to the county park. (See Walk #17)

For an inland return route, follow the footpath along Arroyo Burro Creek inland, crossing the parking lot and heading east (back downcoast) along Cliff Drive. In a short distance, you'll reach the intersection of Las Positas Road and Cliff Drive. At this intersection, head right, ascending the fire road leading through grand oaks up to the bluffs.

Atop the bluffs, bear to your right and begin a counter-clockwise walk around the blufftop. This is the so-called Wilcox Property, where a commercial nursery once stood. You can see many tall pine and eucalyptus trees, as well as some exotic flora gone wild. Santa Barbara conservationists tried twice in the 1980s to convince their fellow citizens to set aside this property as a park, but failed twice (barely) in getting the necessary two-thirds majority at the polls. The property is slated for development.

You'll enjoy great tree-framed coastal views from the bluffs. By following the dirt path that leads along the blufftop, you'll emerge from the Wilcox Property onto Medcliff Road. Follow this a few blocks, which passes the Mesa Lane coastal accessway and continues along the bluffs as Edgewater Way. Turn left on Olive Road, walk two short blocks and turn right on El Camino de la Luz. This road deadends to auto traffic, but you continue eastward over a pedestrian bridge to La Mesa Park, a neighborhood park near the lighthouse. Now join Shoreline Drive and return to where you began at Santa Cruz Boulevard.

[95]

17. Arroyo Burro Beach to Goleta Beach

HIGHLIGHTS: Hope Ranch, More Mesa Beach, Arroyo Burro Beach and Goleta Beach county parks. Isolated beaches reward the walker.
DISTANCE: 4½ miles one way. Parts best at low tide.
TRANSPORTATION: MTD bus. Driving: From Highway 101 in Santa Barbara, exit on Las Positas Road (225) and drive south to its intersection with Cliff Drive and make a right. Arroyo Burro Beach County Park is a short distance on your left.

From Stearns Wharf, here's a prettier route: Follow Cabrillo Boulevard west (up-coast). The boulevard becomes Shoreline Drive, passes Shoreline Park, then turns north to intersect Cliff Drive. Turn left on Cliff to Arroyo Burro County Park.

THIS walk begins at Arroyo Burro Beach County Park. At the turn of the century the Hendry family owned the beach and it was known as "Hendry's." Today some Santa Barbarans refer to it as "Henry's." The beach was officially re-christened Arroyo Burro in 1947 when the state purchased it for $15,000. The park, later given to the county, was named for the creek which empties into the ocean at this point. Arroyo Burro is popular for picnicking, boogie boarding, sunbathing and hang-glider watching.

On the bluffs above the beach is one of the most unique residential communities in America. "Sun-kissed, ocean-washed, mountain-girded, island-guarded" was the breathless description of Hope Ranch gushing forth from real estate brochures of the 1920s.

In this case, the agents were offering more truth than hype. Hope

Ranch was—and still is—one of the most naturally blessed residential areas on the West Coast.

Two of California's most foremost architects, Reginald Johnson and George Washington Smith, put the full power of their craft and imagination to work in the design of many a mansion. Although some of the sumptuous homes had formal gardens, for the most part Hope Ranch residents preferred the natural setting—oak woodland and ocean views. Today, with miles of bridle trails and a private beach club, residents still enjoy the outdoors life.

Hope Ranch had humble beginnings. Thomas Hope, an immigrant from Ireland, acquired 6,000 acres of land for sheep grazing; when the price of wool rose dramatically during the Civil War, Hope became a very wealthy man. He and his wife Delia lived an affluent lifestyle that set the pace for the newcomers who moved to Hope Ranch when it was subdivided.

THE WALK: Head up-coast on Arroyo Burro Beach. The area was once the site of a major Chumash village. Archeological excavations have produced many tools and artifacts. On the high bluffs above is the exclusive community of Hope Ranch. Residents often ride their horses along the surf line.

You'll round a minor point and after two miles or so of beach-walking, pass the red-tiled changing rooms of Hope Ranch Beach Club.

More Mesa Beach follows, one of the most peaceful beaches in the county. Only the buzzing of innumerable flies around the kelp disturbs the tranquility of the serious sunworshippers who bake their hides here. The only public accessway between the two county parks is the dirt path leading up to More Mesa. (See Walk #18)

Beyond More Mesa is another mile of sandy, kelp-strewn beach. The sea cliffs here and in other parts of Santa Barbara have receded three to ten inches per year or roughly 50 feet per century. While this erosion is less than other parts of the world—the White Cliffs of Dover, for example—it's still substantial enough to be a consideration for builders of bluff-top houses.

No, that's not a lighthouse you see in the distance. It's Storke Tower in the center of the University of California at Santa Barbara. As you walk Goleta Beach, you'll round a point and see Goleta Pier.

[97]

In 1981, five ancient cannons were found along Goleta Beach, a half-mile south of Goleta Slough. Pacific storm waves exhumed the cannons, which are believed to be of British origin, circa 1700s. Historians speculate the cannons are from British ships, which once lurked along the coast waiting for the treasure-laden galleons of the Spanish.

Walkers soon arrive at the mouth of Goleta Slough, large tidal mudflats that lie between the UCSB campus and the Santa Barbara Airport. Atascadero Creek empties into the slough, where a great variety of birds, crustaceans and native flora thrive.

The Oak Grove People, who predated the Chumash, lived in the slough area as early as 5000 B.C. When Spanish explorers arrived, they encountered a large group of Chumash living on Mescalitan Island in the center of the slough. At that time the slough was a natural harbor, where the Spanish could anchor their vessels. A wrecked ship stuck in the slough is said to have been the origin of its name; Goleta is the Spanish word for "schooner."

Goleta Landing was built in 1897 and served as a shipping point for Goleta Valley walnuts and citrus. Pioneer families enjoyed boating, fishing, duck hunting and camping on the slough.

Although the slough is smaller than it was before bulldozing and flood control projects, in the 1960s it was saved from a Santa Barbara mayor's pet plan: a speedboat lake surrounded by a racetrack for sports cars.

Wade the shallow. sandy-bottomed slough, resume walking on the sandy beach, and enter Goleta Beach County Park. Goleta Pier's 1,450-foot length (about ¼ mile) is a nice walk in and of itself. It's a popular sport-fishing spot. A seafood restaurant and picnic area are near the pier.

Unpack your picnic, unroll your beach towel and catch some rays, or walk on up-coast to the nearby University of California at Santa Barbara.

18. More Mesa and a Most Mellow Beach

HIGHLIGHTS: Mellow trail through wildlife habitat to Santa Barbara's most tranquil beach.
DISTANCE: One-mile walk, then down a steep path to the beach. If it's not beach weather, or if you're in the mood for a nice walk, take the 3½-mile loop around the mesa suggested below.
INSIDER'S TIPS: Longtime More Mesa activist Dr. Larry Bickford suggests walking around the mesa on winter evenings during the hour before sunset. The black-shouldered kite, marsh hawk and other raptors are quite active in their pursuit of food.
TRANSPORTATION: MTD buses stop at Puente Drive and Hollister. Walk ¾ mile along Puente Drive to Via Huerto. By auto: From upper State Street at its junction with 154 continue along State as it becomes Hollister 1¼ miles to Puente Drive. Turn left on Puente Drive and drive ¾ mile to Vie Huerto on your left. Park along Puente Drive, which is known as Vieja Drive just past Via Huerto.

A second way to enter More Mesa is to continue a short distance along Vieja Drive and walk up Mockingbird Lane to the mesa.

ASK locals about More Mesa and watch the expression on their faces—a smile, a frown, a wink. Smiles will come from those who've found tranquility roaming the bluffs of More Mesa. Frowns may darken the faces of some; developers and their supporters have long wanted to build housing on the mesa and resent the efforts of conservationists and county officials to preserve the land.

The winks might come from those who know that the isolated beach below More Mesa is one of Santa Barbara's secrets; the cleanest and mellowest beach around.

The mesa was part of a large spread, Rancho La Goleta, when rancher Thomas More bought 400 acres in 1857 and began grazing cattle on the land. An enterprising fellow, More noticed natural tar seeping from mesa cliffs, gathered it up and sold it to San Francisco, where the asphaltum was used to pave city streets in the 1860s.

Today, the mesa is known for other natural resources—primarily its bird life. Black-shouldered kites forage the mesa. The population of this bird is on the rebound after habitat destruction and egg collection nearly caused its extinction at the turn of the century.

Other rare birds include the northern harrier and the merlin (a kind of falcon). To the chagrin of developers, the rare, migratory short-eared owl winters on the mesa. "The short-eared owl doesn't pay taxes," scoffed one upset developer, whose project was delayed over environmental concerns.

Naturally, the one-mile walk across More Mesa to the cliff edge, then down a steep path to the beach, is a winner on a sunny day, particularly if your goal is an all-over tan. But don't overlook More Mesa when the weather is bad; its quiet can be enjoyed on the darkest of days.

You can also enjoy More Mesa without even going down to the beach. The property is honeycombed with trails.

More Mesa is the cleanest beach in Santa Barbara County, not because of government maintenance (it gets none) but because beach-goers themselves care deeply about this special place, and patrol it themselves. You can do your part to preserve the quiet beauty of this beach by picking up any trash you find, and leaving no litter behind when you leave.

THE WALK: From Via Huerto, join the dirt path as it ascends steeply for a hundred yards to a wooden fence and row of cypress trees. The path then descends to the relatively flat mesa itself. As you'll notice on your right, not all attempts to keep More Mesa pristine were successful; there are two housing developments on the mesa's northeast corner. The path, joined by other paths connecting from the west, crosses the sweet-smelling, fennel-covered flatlands. Mustard predominates and in springtime covers the bluffs with a blanket of yellow.

At the ocean edge of the mesa is a line of eucalyptus and the dirt path leading down to the beach. The steep path is stabilized by logs. At the bottom is More Mesa Beach, where sunbathers can spread their towels and doze and beach walkers can travel as far up or down the coast as time and tides permit.

Walkers will definitely enjoy the blufftop path leading upcoast along the oceanside edge of More Mesa. The path offers great views of the campus of the University of California at Santa Barbara.

More Mesa Foundation director Dr. Larry Bickford suggests a clockwise route around the periphery of More Mesa. Follow the bluff trail to the first major trail on your right, turning north toward the mountains, then dipping into oak-filled ravines. You'll pass some minor trails then intersect the old Southern Pacific railroad bed; the railroad crossed the mesa in 1887. Beneath the rail route today is a pipeline that carries natural gas from nearby deposits discovered in the 1930s. And the old rail route is a fine hiking trail. A left on the trail will take you through oak woodland to Shoreline Drive and Orchid Drive in a residential area. (This is another good place to begin a More Mesa walk). A right on the trail leads through the oaks along seasonal Atascadero Creek. The "pipeline trail" eventually intersects a profusion of trails. Improvise a route eastward back across the mesa to the trailhead.

19. Beach Combing to Ellwood: Sloughs, Submarines, and Sandy Shores

HIGHLIGHTS: Learn about the unique ecology of a slough, visit the site of the only Japanese attack on the U.S. mainland during W.W. II. Enjoy miles of rarely visited beach.

DISTANCE: 7 miles round trip from Goleta Beach to Coal Oil Preserve, 12 miles round trip to Ellwood Beach Pier.

TRANSPORTATION: MTD bus to the university; begin walking the shore up-coast from here.

By auto: From Highway 101 in Goleta, head south on Ward Memorial Drive (Route 217) for two miles to Goleta Beach County Park. Park in the large beach lot.

AROUND seven o'clock in the evening of February 23, 1942, while most Southern Californians were listening to President Roosevelt's fireside chat on the radio, strange explosions were heard near Goleta. In the first (and only) attack on U.S. soil since the War of 1812, a Japanese submarine surfaced off the rich oil field on Ellwood Beach, twelve miles north of Santa Barbara, and lobbed sixteen shells into the tidewater field.

"Their marksmanship was poor," asserted Lawrence Wheeler, proprietor of a roadside inn near the oil fields. Most observers agreed with Wheeler, who added there was no panic among his dinner patrons, "We immediately blacked out the place," he said. "One shell landed about a quarter-mile from here and the concussion shook the building, but nobody was scared much."

The unmolested, unhurried Japanese gunners were presumably aiming at the oil installations and the coast highway bridge over the Southern Pacific tracks. Tokyo claimed the raid "a great military success" though the incredibly bad marksmen managed to inflict only $500 worth of damage. The submarine disappeared into the night, leaving behind air raid sirens, a jumpy population and lower real estate values.

The walk along Goleta Beach to Ellwood Oil Field is interesting for more than historical reasons. On the way to the Oil Field/Battlefield, you'll pass tidepools, shifting sand dunes, and the Devereux Slough. The slough is a unique intertidal ecosystem and is protected for teaching and research purposes by Coal Oil Point Preserve.

THE WALK: Proceed up-coast (west—remember, you're in confusing Santa Barbara County where the coast stretches east to west). In a quarter-mile you'll reach a stretch of coast called the Main Campus Reserve Area, where you'll find the Goleta Slough. The same month the Japanese bombed Ellwood Beach, Santa Barbara voters approved a bond issue to buy land around the Goleta Slough, and a modern airport was constructed on the site of the old cow pasture/airfield. The slough, host to native and migratory waterfowl, is a remnant of a wetland that was once much more extensive.

Continue up-beach past the handsome sandstone cliffs. Occasionally a high tide may force you to detour atop the bluffs through the UCSB campus to avoid getting wet. A mile and a half from the county park, you'll round Goleta Point and head due west. You pass a nice tidepool area; judging from the number of college students, it is well studied.

Two more miles of beachcombing brings you to Coal Oil Point. You'll want to explore the nature reserve here. (Please observe all posted warnings; this is a very fragile area.)

The dunes are the first component of the reserve encountered on the seaward side. Sandy hillocks are stabilized with grasses and rushes. Salty sand provides little nourishment yet the hardy seaside flora manage to survive, settling as close to the water as the restless Pacific will permit. The dunes keep the plants from blowing away and the plants return the favor for the dunes.

Footprints of lizards and mice and miniscule tracks of beetles can be seen tacking this way and that over the sand. The dunes' surface records the lightest pressure of the smallest feet. Sometimes one set of animal tracks intersects another in a pattern suggesting the demise of one animal and dinner for another.

Pick up the trail over the dunes on the east side of the reserve. The fennel-lined trail passes under cypress trees and climbs a bluff above the slough to a road on the reserve's perimeter. It's a good place to get "the big picture" of the slough, a unique ecosystem. Something like an estuary, a slough has a mixture of fresh and salt water, but an estuary has a more stable mixture. The water gets quite salty at Devereux Slough, with little freshwater flushing.

At the slough, bird-watchers rhapsodize over snowy egrets and great blue herons, black-bellied plovers and western sandpipers. Avid bird-watchers flock to the slough for birdathons—marathon bird-sighting competitions.

In addition to the scores of native and migratory species, birds affectionately known by their watchers as "vagrants"—lost birds who have no business in the area—often visit the slough. If you're the type who carries a copy of *Petersen's Guide* in your day pack, you'll spend the rest of the day here and there's no point in urging you to hike on. For the rest of you, it's on to Ellwood.

Return to the beach and continue walking up the coast. Sometimes horses gallop over the dunes, suggesting Peter O'Toole and Omar Sharif's meeting in *Lawrence of Arabia* . . . except there's oil on the beach, as you'll readily notice when you look at your feet. In two miles you'll pass under an old barnacle-covered oil drilling platform and enter Ellwood Oil Field. Here the Japanese fired shots heard 'round the world . . . and missed.

20. Sun and Sand in Summerland

HIGHLIGHTS: Fun and sun in the beach and beach community south of Santa Barbara.
DISTANCE: 5 miles round trip from Lookout County Park to Biltmore Beach and Hotel. Best at low tide.
TRANSPORTATION: MTD bus to Summerland Post Office. Walk south on Evans Road to Lookout County Park.
  By auto: From Highway 101 in Summerland, take the Summerland exit and turn oceanward to Lookout County Park.

ONE might guess Summerland was named for the weather, but the name was taken from Spiritualist literature—something to do with the Second Heaven of Spiritualism. A century ago, Spiritualists pitched their tents on the tiny lots here, just south of Santa Barbara.

In the waters here, the first offshore oil platform in the Western hemisphere was erected in 1896. Soon, more than three hundred wells were pumping oil from Pleistocene rocks at depths of 100 to 800 feet, an insignificant depth by today's standards.

Oil attracted far more people to Summerland than Spiritualism and soon the air was heavy with the smell of gas and oil. It was said that free illumination came easy—one simply pounded a pipe in the ground 'til reaching natural gas, and lit a match. Liberty Hall, the Spiritualists' community center, glowed with divine light and for a time Summerland became known as the "White City."

This walk travels due west along sandy Summerland Beach, rounds some rocky points, and concludes at the narrow beach in front of the famed Biltmore Hotel.

THE WALK: At Lookout County Park is a picnic area and a monument commemorating the first offshore oil rig. A well- marked ramp leads to the beach. From Lookout (Summerland) Beach, a sea wall extends ¾ mile west to Fernald Point. At high tide, you may wish to walk atop it, but you'll have to battle some brush. You soon pass a pretty little cove, bounded on the far side by Fernald Point, formed by a fan delta deposited at the mouth of Romero Creek.

Around the point, as you approach Montecito, you'll see the higher parts of the Santa Ynez Mountains on the north skyline and the overturned beds of sandstone near the peaks. There are no official public beaches in Montecito, but most of the shoreline receives public use: Fernald-Sharks Cove is the first beach you travel, then Miramar Beach below the Miramar Hotel. "Miramar-by-the-Sea" has been a popular watering place since the completion of the Southern Pacific railroad line in 1901. The hotel, with its finely landscaped grounds and blue-roofed bungalows, used to be a passenger stop.

In another quarter-mile, you'll begin hiking across Montecito's third beach, Hammonds, popular with surfers. Hammonds Meadows on the bluffs above the beach is a former Chumash habitation and a poten- tially rich archaeological dig. Although it was recently placed on the National Register of Historic Places, it's being developed.

Up-coast from Hammonds you'll pass a number of fine homes and arrive at narrow Biltmore Beach, frequented by the rich and beautiful. Opposite the beach is the magnificent Biltmore Hotel, built in 1927.

21. Beach and Butterflies at El Capitan and Refugio State Beaches

HIGHLIGHTS: Clusters of Monarch butterflies. Pleasant beaches and bluffs of two state beaches.
DISTANCE: 6-mile round trip walk from El Capitan to Refugio State Beach.
TRANSPORTATION: From Highway 101, 19 miles up-coast from Santa Barbara, take the El Capitan State Beach exit. Park in one of the day use areas. There's a $5 state park day use fee, which is honored at Refugio and Gaviota State Beaches also.

MONARCH butterflies and mellow beaches are the highlights of this coast walk north of Santa Barbara. Autumn, when the crowds have thinned and the butterflies have arrived, is a particularly fine time to roam the coast from El Capitan State Beach to Refugio State Beach.

El Capitan is a narrow beach at the mouth of El Capitan Creek. Shading the creek is a woodland of coast live oak and sycamore. During autumn, Monarch butterflies congregate and breed in the trees here. (Ask park rangers where the Monarchs cluster in large numbers.)

The butterflies have a distinctive coloring—brownish-red wings with black veins. The outer edges of their wings are dark brown with white and yellow spots. During October and November, the woodland of El Capitan Creek offers the twin delights of falling autumn leaves and fluttering butterflies.

"El Capitan" refers to Captain José Francisco de Ortega, a rotund Spanish Army officer who served as trail scout for the Portolá expedition. When he retired from service to the Crown in 1795, he owed the army money and offered to square things by raising cattle. The government granted him his chosen land: a coastal strip, two miles wide and twenty-five miles long extending from just east of Point Conception to Refugio Canyon. He called his land Nuestra Señora del Refugio, "Our Lady of Refuge." Alas, Captain Ortega's retirement was short-lived; he died three years later and was buried at the Santa Barbara Mission.

Beach, bluff and bike trails link El Capitan and Refugio State Beaches. Depending on the tide, you can usually travel up-coast along El Capitan Beach as far as Coral Canyon Beach. Then you can join the bluff trails or the bike path, which is also open to hikers, for the balance of the trip to Refugio Beach.

El Capitan and Refugio are popular beach campgrounds and nice places to spend a weekend.

THE WALK: Descend one of the paths or staircases to the shore, then head up-coast along the mixed sandy and rocky beach. Sea cliffs are steep here, because they are constantly being cut back by wave erosion. At Coral Beach, the tides often discourage beach-walking, so head up to the bluffs and follow the bike path.

Refugio State Beach, at the mouth of Refugio Canyon, is a rocky beach with tidepools. Turn around here, or continue beach walking up-coast (it's 10 more miles to Gaviota State Beach) for as long as time and tides permit.

22. Glorious End of Southern California: Point Conception

HIGHLIGHTS: Unique ecology, dramatic views.
DISTANCE: From Jalama County Park to just-short of Pt. Conception is a 10-mile round trip walk.
TRANSPORTATION: Jalama County Park is located 20 miles southwest of Lompoc off Highway 1. From Highway 101, near Gaviota, exit on Highway 1 north and proceed 14 miles to Jalama Road. Turn left and go 14 miles through some beautiful ranch country to the county park. There is a park day use fee.

AT Point Conception, the western-running shoreline of Southern California turns sharply northward and heralds a number of changes: a colder Pacific, foggier days, cooler air. Ecological differences between the north and south coasts are illustrated by the differing marine life occupying the two sections. Point Conception serves as a line of demarcation between differing species of polyps, abalone, crabs and limpets. Climatically, geographically and sociologically, it can be argued that Southern California ends at Point Conception.

This walk takes you along a pristine section of beach and retraces the route of the De Anza Trail, a trail lost to most hikers for over 200 years. The De Anza Trail was the route of Juan Bautista De Anza Expedition of 1775-76, which brought 240 colonists from Mexico across the Colorado Desert and up the coast to found the city of San Francisco.

Historically, the Anza Trail is much better documented than the

Lewis and Clark or other trails that opened up the west. This is due to the meticulous diary-keeping of Anza and the expedition's chaplain, Father Font.

On February 26, 1776, the Anza Expedition reached an Indian village called Rancheria Nueva, just east of Point Conception. Father Font noted the generosity of the Indians, praised their well-crafted baskets and stone cups, and concluded that the Indians would be good recruits for future missions.

This beach walk leaves from Jalama County Park, the only genuinely public access point anywhere near Point Conception. If the tide is right (be sure to consult a tide table), you can walk to within about a half-mile of the Point.

The coast between Gaviota State Park and Jalama County Park is divided between two huge ranches: the Hollister Ranch, which controls the land between Gaviota State Park and Point Conception and the Bixby Ranch, which occupies the land between Point Conception and Jalama.

Travel writer Frank Riley has facetiously remarked that "Anza, Father Font, Father Junipero Serra and Jesus himself would have to carry bail money to round Point Conception by land today." Riley is right; public outrage will ultimately see to it that some sort of trail or bike path gives the public access to the coast, but in the meantime be warned that the Bixby Ranch and Hollister Ranch are among the most aggressively anti-coastal-access private property holders in the state.

Remember to keep to the beach and don't walk the inland trails onto ranch land.

THE WALK: Before heading south over the splendid sand dunes, check the tide table at the park store or at the entry kiosk. As you walk down-coast, you'll soon realize that although Jalama County Park is not on the main Los Angeles-San Francisco thoroughfare, two groups have found it and claimed it as their own—surfers and surf fishermen.

Jalama County Park includes only about ½ mile of shoreline, so you soon walk beyond the park boundary. The sandy beach narrows and gives way to rockier shore. Offshore, on the rocky reefs, seals linger.

They seem to enjoy basking in the sun and getting doused by the breakers. Depending on the tide, you'll encounter a number of sea walls. The smooth tops of the sea walls make a good trail. "1934" is the date imbedded in the concrete walls.

Occasionally, Southern Pacific railroad tracks come into view, though with the crashing of the breakers, you can barely hear the passing trains. Since there are no public roads along this section of coast, walking or looking out a train window are the only ways to see this special country. Halfway through your walk, after some lazy bends, the coastline heads almost due south and the Point Conception Coast Guard Reservation comes into view.

A bit more than a half-mile from the lighthouse, you'll run out of beach to walk; passage is blocked by waves crashing against the point. Stay away from the lighthouse and Coast Guard Reservation; visitors are not welcome. A blufftop road and a number of cow trails lead toward the lighthouse, established by the federal government in 1855; however, these routes cross private ranch land and may not be used.

23. Secret Ocean Beach Park

HIGHLIGHTS: Mouth of Santa Ynez River, wild and windy beach.
DISTANCE: From Ocean Beach County Park to Pt. Pedernales is 7 miles round trip.
TRANSPORTATION: North of Santa Barbara, just past the Gaviota Pass tunnel, exit Highway 101 onto Highway 1 and proceed toward Lompoc. Join Highway 246 heading west toward Vandenberg and drive about 8 miles out of Lompoc to signed Ocean Park Road on your right. Another sign reads: Ocean Park/Coastal Access. Turn right onto Ocean Park Road and drive a mile (don't be discouraged by the ugly approach) past some railroad sidings and freight cars to Ocean Beach County Park parking lot.

Ocean Beach is often very windy, so dress accordingly. The beach is wide and passable at either high or low tide; it's easier at low tide, however, so consult a tide table.

PSSSSSST! Want to know a secret? A military secret?

There's a five-mile long beach in the middle of Vandenberg Air Force Base no one knows, where no one goes.

Vandenberg Air Force Base in Santa Barbara County occupies more Southern California coastline than any other private landholder or government agency. The base encompasses some 35 miles of coastline—about the same amount of shore that belongs to Orange County—and public access is severely restricted.

Happily, Santa Barbara County's Ocean Beach County Park puts a small part of Vandenberg's beach within reach. The park's facilities and picnic ground have recently been upgraded, though the beach itself is as windswept and wild as ever.

Next to the county park is a large, shallow lagoon at the mouth of the Santa Ynez River. Most of this river's flow is captured high in the Santa Ynez Mountains by a series of dams and Cachuma Lake. By the time drought-plagued Santa Barbara and Lompoc Valley farmers take their allotted river water, not much of the Santa Ynez makes it to the Pacific. Today, looking at the river mouth, it's hard to imagine that the Santa Ynez River once supported the largest run of spawning steelhead trout in Southern California before Cachuma Lake Dam was built in the 1950s.

Still, there's enough freshwater, mixed with some Pacific saltwater, to form a 400-acre marsh back of the river mouth. Bird-watchers will especially enjoy spending some time exploring the wetlands. Near the sandbar at the river mouth, birders will spot gulls and sandpipers and perhaps even a nesting colony of the endangered least tern. Patrolling the estuary's cattail-lined tidal channels are mallards, canvas back and ruddy ducks. On the mudflat areas are such migrating shorebirds as willets and long-billed curlews.

After you've visited the estuary, it's time to hit the beach. This day hike heads south along windswept Ocean Beach toward Point Arguello. However, before you reach the point, you'll be stopped by another—Point Pedernales—named by the 1769 Portolá expedition when flints, or *pedernales*, were found here. Point Pedernales is about the end of the public beach; besides, the surf crashing against the point is nature's way of telling you to turn around.

THE WALK: Hike over the low dunes, dotted with clumps of European beach grass, ice plant and hottentot fig, toward the ocean. You'll pass a couple of pilings sticking out of the sand—the remains of an old fishing pier. Continue over the sands, sprinkled with sea rocket and sand verbena, to the shore. You could walk a mile north on public beach (though sometimes the Santa Ynez River mouth is difficult to ford), but this day hike heads south.

After a mile of walking down-coast, the cliffs rise above you and add to a splendid feeling of isolation. Vandenberg Air Force Base, occupying the cliffs above, used to be the Army's Camp Cooke until the Army turned it over to the Air Force in 1957 and it was renamed for Air Force General Hoyt S. Vandenberg. Atlas ICBMs, Discoverer I, the first polar-orbited satellite, and missiles of all kinds have been launched from the base during the last three decades.

Because this stretch of coast bends so far westward, it's ideal for launches into a polar orbit. Look on the world map and you can see there's nothing but empty ocean between here and the South Pole; if a launch fails, the debris will fall on water, not land.

You can see some of the launch pads and towers as you continue down-coast. You'll also sight dramatic Point Arguello, overlooking the treacherous waters that have doomed many a ship. One of the worst accidents in U.S. Naval history occurred in 1923 when seven destroyers ran aground just north of the point. In the dense fog of the Santa Barbara Channel, the ships got off-course. Officers refused to heed the new-fangled radio equipment or Radio Directional Finder (RDF) stations onshore and instead plotted their course by "dead reckoning" which proved to be dead wrong.

One of the minor reefs of Point Pedernales will no doubt stop your forward progress. If you have a pair of binoculars, you might be able to spots some harbor seals sunning themselves on the rocks below the point.

24. Point Sal

HIGHLIGHTS: Wild and remote beach, dramatic point for observing seals and sea lions.
DISTANCE: From the state beach to the point, it's 5 miles. It's possible to extend your walk quite a bit by continuing up-coast to Nipomo Dunes.
TRANSPORTATION: From Highway 101 in Santa Maria, exit on Betteravia Road. Proceed west past a commercial strip and then out into the sugar beet fields. Betteravia Road twists north. About eight miles from Highway 101, turn left on Brown Road. Five miles of driving on Brown Road (watch for cows wandering along the road) brings you to a signed junction; leftward is a ranch road, but you bear right on Point Sal Road, partly paved, partly dirt washboard (impassable in wet weather). Follow this road 5 miles to its end at the parking area above Point Sal State Beach.

Be advised that Point Sal Road is sometimes closed during the rainy season. The Air Force sometimes closes the road for short periods during its missile launches.

WHEN your eye travels down a map of Central California coast, you pause on old and familiar friends—the state beaches at San Simeon, Morro Bay, and Pismo Beach. Usually overlooked is another state beach—remote Point Sal, a nub of land north of Vandenberg Air Force Base and south of the Guadalupe Dunes. Windy Point Sal is a wall of bluffs rising 50 to 100 feet above the rocky shore. The water is crystal-clear, and the blufftops provide a fine spot to watch the boisterous seals and sea lions.

Point Sal was named by explorer Vancouver in 1792 for Hermenegildo Sal, at that time commandante of San Francisco. The state purchased the land in the 1940s. There are no facilities whatsoever at the beach, so remember, if you pack it in, pack it out.

This walk travels Point Sal State Beach, then takes to the bluffs above rocky reefs. At low tide, you can pass around or over the reefs; at high tide the only passage is along the bluff trail. Both marine life and land life can be observed from the bluff trail.

The trail system in the Point Sal area is in rough condition. The narrow bluff trails should not be undertaken by novice hikers, the weak-kneed or those afraid of heights. Families with small children and less-experienced trekkers will enjoy beachcombing and tidepool-watching opportunities at Point Sal and the pleasure of discovering this out-of-the-way beach.

THE WALK: From the parking area, follow one of the short steep trails down to the beautiful crescent-shaped beach. Hike up-coast along the windswept beach. In $^1/_3$ mile, you'll reach the end of the beach at a rocky reef, difficult to negotiate at high tide. A second reef, encountered shortly after the first, is equally difficult. Atop this reef, there's a rope secured to an iron stake to aid your descent to the beach below. The rope is also helpful in ascending the reef on your return.

Unless it's very low tide, you'll want to begin following the narrow bluff trail above the reefs. The trail arcs westward with the coast, occasionally dipping down to rocky and romantic pocket beaches sequestered between reefs.

About 1½ miles from the trailhead, you'll descend close to shore and begin boulder-hopping. After a few hundred yards of boulder-hopping, you'll begin to hear the bark of sea lions and get an aviator's view of Lion Rock, where the gregarious animals bask in the sun.

Your trek continues on a pretty decent bluff trail, which dips down near a sea lion haul-out. (Please don't approach or disturb these creatures.) You'll then ascend rocky Point Sal. From the point, you'll view the Guadalupe Dunes complex to the north and the sandy beaches of Vandenberg Air Force Base to the south. Before returning the same way, look for red-tailed hawks riding the updrafts and admire the ocean boiling up over the reefs.

Energetic hikers can follow a trail which passes behind Point Sal, joins a sandy road, and descends to a splendid, two-mile-long, sandy beach north of the point. This unnamed beach is almost always deserted except for a few fishermen and lots of pelicans.

Short Walks and Special Stops

Carpinteria State Beach

Carpinteria residents have long boasted they have "the safest beach in the world" because although the surf can be large, it breaks far out and there's no undertow. As early as 1920, visitors reported "the 'Hawaiian diversion of surf-board riding."

The beach is still popular with surfers, particularly an area called "the tarpits" at the south end of the beach. The state beach also attracts swimmers, sunbathers and a lot of campers to its large campground.

You can enjoy a short walk south along the state beach to City Bluff Park or head up-coast from the state beach to Carpinteria City Beach.

TRANSPORTATION: MTD bus to Linden Avenue. Walk a mile south to the beach.

By auto, take the Linden Avenue exit and drive to the beach.

Summerland Beach

Walk #20 describes beachcombing from Lookout County Park up-coast to the Biltmore, but you can also take a short walk down-coast for a mile or so. This stretch of sand is sometimes used to exercise the polo ponies from the nearby Santa Barbara Polo Club. It's a beautiful sight to see them galloping along the surfline.

TRANSPORTATION: MTD bus to Summerland Post Office. Walk south on Evans Road to Lookout County Park.

By auto, from Highway 101 in Summerland, take the Summerland exit and turn oceanward to Lookout County Park.

Gaviota State Park

Camping, picnicking and fishing are some of the attractions of this mellow state park. From the fishing pier, tides permitting, you can walk south to Alcatraz Beach, where you'll encounter some great tidepools.

TRANSPORTATION: Follow Highway 101 thirty-five miles up-coast from Santa Barbara to Gaviota State Park.

COUNTRY

*That anybody should undertake a jaunt of a hundred and
fifty miles or so on foot for the pleasure of walking was
unthinkable by the conventional western mind; but I was
already familiar with the strong points of tripping afoot
and the lure of that splendid chain of mountains back of
Santa Barbara . . . To motor there seemed out of key with
such a land, though thousands do it; and besides, motoring
is expensive. No, for me 'The footpath way' with kodak
over my shoulder, a pocketful of dried figs, and freedom
from care.*

—CHARLES FRANCIS SAUNDERS
Under the Sky in California, (1913)

Country

BOTANIST/Southern California outdoors writer Charles Francis Saunders was one of the first to recognize the primordial joys of hiking the rugged chains of mountains back of Santa Barbara. This land of great gorges, sandstone cliffs and wide blue sky was—and is—very special.

Even today, most of Santa Barbara County is uninhabited, unsullied. Some 630,000 acres of canyons and mountains are government land, within the boundaries of Los Padres National Forest. Santa Barbara County's park system has also preserved some special places.

Behind Santa Barbara are the Santa Ynez Mountains, ranging from 2,000 to 4,000 feet high. The mountains extend about fifty miles west from Matilija Canyon near Ojai to Gaviota Canyon.

Some of the very best hiking in Southern California is along trails through the mountain canyons right behind Santa Barbara and Montecito. Along with the coast and the city, the countryside has long been an attractive destination for visitors and residents alike. By the turn of the century, the Hot Springs Hotel in Hot Springs Canyon was an internationally famed destination—more exclusive than Baden-Baden and other fine European resorts.

And when visitors weren't taking the healing waters they were tramping through the countryside. Even the Santa Barbara Chamber of Commerce promoted hiking and horseback riding in the local mountains.

At first glance on a summer's day, the Santa Ynez Mountains seem smothered with a formless gray mass of brush. On closer inspection, the range reveals much more charm. Antiquarian oaks and sycamores line the canyons and a host of seasonal creeks wash the hillsides. In spring, the chaparral blooms and adds frosty whites and blues to the gray-green plants. The mountains look particularly inviting after the first winter rains. On upper peaks, rain sometimes turns to snow.

The network of trails generally follow streams to the top of the range. They start in lush canyon bottoms, zigzag up the hot, dry canyon walls, and follow rock ledges to the crest. Many of the trails intersect El Camino Cielo (the sky road), which follows the mountain crest. From the top, enjoy sweeping views of the Pacific and Channel Islands, the city and coastal plain.

From the viewpoints, hikers can decipher Santa Barbara sometime's confusing orientation; that is to say, the east-west direction of the coastline and the mountain ranges. Even many long-time Californians are amused by looking south to the ocean. By all means, consider taking along along a map—the Auto Club's Santa Barbara County map is a good one—to help get oriented.

Back of the Santa Ynez Mountains are several more mountain ranges in what geologists call the Transverse Ranges Geomorphic Province, the government calls Los Padres National Forest, and most locals call the Santa Barbara Backcountry.

During the first decades of this century, the backcountry was called the Santa Barbara Forest Reserve. In later years, acreage was added and subtracted, with the backcountry finally coming under the jurisdiction of Los Padres National Forest in 1938.

More than 1,600 miles of trail range through the various districts of Los Padres National Forest. Nearly half of this trail system winds through the area we call the Santa Barbara Backcountry. Some of these trails have been in use for a century while others—Chumash Indian routes—were in use for many, many centuries.

Today, thanks to local hikers, conservation organizations, county and federal rangers, Santa Barbara has more miles of easily accessible trail than any other community in Southern California. There's a trail waiting to take you wherever you want to go.

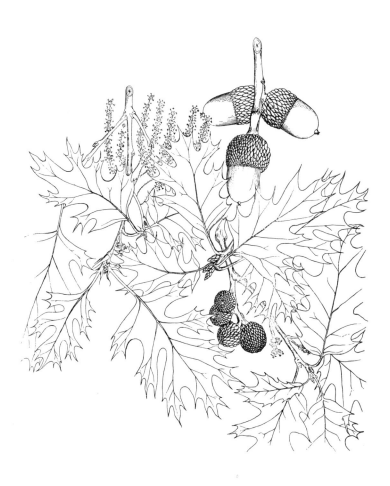

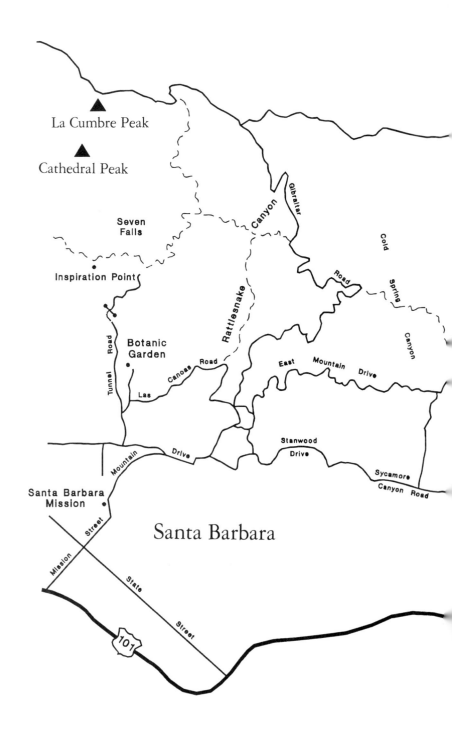

Santa Ynez Mountains

Foothill Trails

Montecito Peak

Romero
Saddle

San

Ysidro

Canyon

Hot
Springs

Romero

Canyon

Canyon

Hot Springs

Road

Road

Romero

Canyon

Valley

East

Drive

Mill

Ysidro

Montecito

Olive

San

Sheffield

25. Romero Canyon

HIGHLIGHTS: Romero Canyon Trail is the most easterly of the delightful Santa Ynez Mountains footpaths back of Santa Barbara. Oaks and sycamores shade a year-round creek and a tranquil trail.

DISTANCE: The shorter hike described below is a 6-mile loop through Romero Canyon with a 1,400-foot elevation gain. The longer loop is 11 miles with a 2,300-foot gain.

TRANSPORTATION: From Highway 101 in Montecito, a few miles down-coast from Santa Barbara, exit on Sheffield Drive. Turn right on Sheffield Drive, which briefly parallels the freeway, then swings sharply left (north) toward the Santa Ynez Mountains. Drive 1½ miles to East Valley Road. Turn left, proceed 50 yards, then make an almost immediate right on Romero Canyon Road. A half-mile along, be sure to veer right at a fork in the road, and continue another mile farther to Bella Vista Road. Turn right and continue a quarter-mile to a red steel gate on the left side of the road. Park in a safe manner alongside Bella Vista Road.

ROMERO Canyon was named for the Romero family, whose first members came to the Santa Barbara area more than two hundred years ago. Juan Romero was a soldier with Governor Felipe de Neve (first resident governor of California) and Captain José Francisco Ortega, who helped found El Presidio Real de Santa Barbara in 1782.

Later Romeros living up in the canyon that took their name include Apolinario, who resided near the mouth of the canyon; Mariano, who settled way up the canyon; and Benito, who lived in a rugged part of the canyon that some thought *ni servia para criar cachorra,* not fit even to raise lizards.

One meaning of romero in Spanish is "pilgrim" and pilgrims of several levels of hiking ability will enjoy a walk through Romero Canyon. Families with small children will enjoy sauntering along its lower creekside stretches. More serious hikers will utilize fire roads to make a moderately graded loop through the canyon, while hikers in top form will trek all the way to El Camino Cielo (the sky road) which offers sweeping views from the crest of the Santa Ynez Mountains.

THE WALK: Slip around the red gate and head up-canyon on the fire road. After a quarter-mile of travel, you'll cross a concrete bridge near Romero Creek. A half-mile from the trailhead, you'll cross the creek again. Just after the creek crossing, join unsigned Romero Canyon Trail on your left. Grasses and sedges, bay laurel and a tangle of vines line the creek. Even during drought years, Romero Canyon is surprisingly lush.

Ascending moderately to steeply, the trail crosses the creek a couple more times, then climbs briskly via a quarter-mile of switchbacks to a signed four-way trail intersection.

LOWER LOOP: Turn right where the trail intersects the dirt road and begin your 4-mile descent. After 2 miles of walking, the road offers views of Montecito estates and the coastline, Anacapa and Santa Cruz Islands. The road intersects Romero Canyon Trail one-half mile from the trailhead.

UPPER LOOP: Follow signed Romero Trail, which climbs quite steeply over loose shale slopes to the head of the canyon. The trail crests at the top of the Santa Ynez Mountains, about 3,000 feet in elevation. Coastline views are good but the crest here has been scarred by off-road vehicles. From the crest, the trail descends through a brushy, narrow draw toward Camino Cielo. The trail parallels this dirt road for a short ways, then descends to it. Follow Camino Cielo ½ mile west to a water tank and the unsigned fire road leading into Romero Canyon. Follow this fire road, which makes a long loop south, then east, then north before dropping into Romero Canyon at the above-mentioned four-way trail intersection.

26. San Ysidro Canyon

HIGHLIGHTS: Along San Ysidro Creek you encounter a beautiful oak woodland. With mighty oaks in the foreground and impressive rock formations in the background, it is a striking scene. During years of normal rainfall, hikers heap rocks to make shallow swimming and wading pools.

DISTANCE: From the trailhead at East Mountain Drive to the pools at the bottom of San Ysidro Canyon is about a three-mile round trip with a very slight elevation gain. San Ysidro Trail then climbs rather steeply out of the canyon. Figure 8 miles round trip with a 2,900-foot elevation gain.

INSIDER'S TIPS: Truly decadent hikers will make reservations for the sumptuous Sunday brunch at San Ysidro Ranch located very close to the trailhead.

TRANSPORTATION: From Highway 101 in Montecito, take the San Ysidro Road offramp. Drive north on San Ysidro a mile to East Valley Road, turn right and drive a mile to Park Lane, which appears on the left just after crossing San Ysidro Creek. Turn left on Park Lane and in a half-mile veer left onto East Mountain Dive, which passes through a residential neighborhood to the trailhead. The signed trailhead is just opposite San Ysidro Stables. Parking is along East Mountain Drive.

SAN Ysidro Trail is attractive and typical of Santa Barbara's foothill trails. It's suitable for several levels of hiking ability. Families with small children will enjoy sauntering along its lower creekside stretches. The more serious hiker will enjoy sweating up the switch-backs to Camino Cielo, the Sky Road.

THE WALK: The trail, lined with sea fig, bougainvillea, and other exotic plants, parallels a driveway for a short time, passes a couple houses, then becomes a dirt road. Continue up the dirt road and look up occasionally at the handsome Coldwater sandstone formations above you. To your left across the creek is "the gateway," a popular rock-climbing area. After a half-mile's travel, you'll pass two signed connector trails, which lead to canyons on either side of San Ysidro. To the east is Old Pueblo Trail; to the west, Colonel McMenemy Trail.

San Ysidro Trail continues along the bottom of the narrow, snaky canyon. In the springtime, the path may be brightened with blossoms.

As you meander through the woodland, keep your eye out for some of San Ysidro Creek's pools. Look for a large pool on your left, just before the trail ascends into the upper canyon.

Those hikers heading for the upper stretches of San Ysidro Canyon will leave the creek behind and follow the steep rocky trail. Along one length of trail, pipes serve as handrails and you'll feel as though you're walking the precarious Angel's Landing in Zion National Park rather than this supposedly gentle path through the Santa Ynez Mountains. (The rails really aren't necessary.) The trail continues along a rocky ledge, finds more solid ground, then crosses over the west side of the canyon.

You'll continue marching through the chaparral up long, steep switchbacks. During the ascent, the geologically inclined will look up at the Matilija sandstone of the gray-white Coldwater sandstone formation, which has been wind-sculpted into striking cliffs and bluffs. When you reach East Camino Cielo, return the way you came.

27. Hot Springs Canyon

HIGHLIGHTS: Ruins of the fabled Hot Springs Hotel, a nostalgic look at Santa Barbara's Great Resort Era. Panoramic views of Santa Barbara, Montecito and the Pacific.

DISTANCE: From Hot Springs Road to the Hot Springs Hotel ruins, it's a 3½-mile round trip with a 700-foot elevation gain. Looping through Cold Spring Canyon makes a 7-mile round trip with a 1,100-foot elevation gain.

TRANSPORTATION: From U.S. 101 in Montecito, just down the coast from Santa Barbara, exit on Olive Mill Road, which, after intersecting Alston Drive, continues as Hot Springs Road. Three miles from U.S. 101, you'll reach Mountain Drive. Turn left and proceed a quarter-mile to the trailhead, which is on the right side of the road and is marked by a Montecito Trails Foundation sign. Park in a safe manner alongside the road.

One of our favorite resorts was the Sulphur or Hot Springs, situated some five or six miles from Santa Barbara, to the southward. The springs would make the fortune of any town in the United States, but here are left alone and deserted, visited only by the native sick or the American sojourner in Santa Barbara. They are remarkably, and very romantically, situated; sequestered from human habitation and almost inaccessible save to the pedestrian.

—WALTER MURRAY, 1847
Narrative of a California Volunteer

BY the time the first New York Volunteers arrived in Santa Barbara in 1847, the "conquest of California" was complete. The war with Mexico was over. While garrisoned in Santa Barbara, one Army

volunteer, Walter Murray, seemed to have spent most of his enlist-
ment touring the Santa Barbara Backcountry and recording his
enthusiastic descriptions in a journal. Particularly impressive to Murray was a pretty canyon aptly named Hot Springs for the sulfurous
waters that gushed into inviting bath-size pools.

"I never yet came across a more picturesque sight, nor do I expect
to in the future," Murray wrote. A decade after Murray's bubbly
report, Wilbur Curtiss made his way to Santa Barbara—for health
reasons, as the story goes. Curtiss took the cure and left us a story
chock-full of cliches: He was suffering from an incurable disease. His
doctors gave him but six months to live. Then one day he met a 110-
year-old Indian who attributed his longevity to some secret springs.
Curtiss bathed in the springs and experienced a miracle cure.

Or so the story goes. . . .

Fable or not, Curtiss soon felt well enough to file a homestead
claim on Hot Springs Canyon and begin its commercial development.

By the early 1880s, the homestead became the property of wealthy
Montecitans who built a three-story wooden hotel at the springs.
Rates were $2 a day, $10 a week, including the baths. Guests enjoyed a
library, a billiards room and a well-stocked wine cellar. Another
attraction was hiking: Trails meandered around the hillsides and
provided excellent panoramas of Santa Barbara and the Channel
Islands.

By the turn of the century, the Hot Springs Hotel was more
exclusive than Baden-Baden and other fine European resorts. It was
said only those with seven-digit incomes felt at ease in the healing
waters.

The hotel burned down in 1920, and a small, but still quite posh
clubhouse was built on the site. The new spa was even more exclusive: Membership was limited to 17 Montecito estate owners who
also controlled the Montecito Water Co. Members would telephone
the caretaker, tell him to draw a bath, then arrive a short while later
by limousine. The club burned down in the 1964 Coyote Fire.

Since then, Hot Springs Canyon and its hot pools have been
accessible to the less-affluent. Hot Springs Trail—the old stagecoach
road—leads to the ruins of the resort. Condition and temperature of
the two hot pools vary, so hikers should use their best judgement

when deciding whether to take the plunge. In recent times, there has been some conflict between the local water company and hot spring devotees. Walkers should be on their very best behavior and respect the private property and pipelines belonging to the water company.

THE WALK: The trail climbs moderately through a wooded area, skirting some baronial estates. The first few hundred yards of Hot Springs Trail might give you the impression you're on the wrong trail because it crosses and parallels some private driveways. However, keep following the path with the aid of some strategically placed Montecito Trails Foundation signs.

After a quarter-mile of travel, you'll leave the villas behind. The trail veers right, dips into the canyon, crosses Hot Springs Creek and joins a dirt road. The dirt road passes under the embrace of antiquarian oaks, then begins climbing moderately to steeply along the east side of Hot Springs Canyon. Notice the stone culverts and the handsome stone retaining walls as you walk up the old coach road.

A mile's travel along the old road brings you to a junction. A left at the junction puts you on a power-line road that climbs over to Cold Spring Canyon. Stay right, and another quarter-mile of hiking brings you to the ruins of the Montecito Hot Springs Club. Some stone steps and foundations are about all that's left of the exclusive club.

Nearby, some exotic flora thrive—bamboo, agave and geraniums, as well as palm, banana and avocado trees—remnants of the landscaped gardens that surrounded the spa during its glory days.

You can return the same way, or follow one of two routes to Cold Spring Canyon. You may double back to the above-mentioned road junction and ascend with the power-line road to the ridge separating Hot Springs Canyon from Cold Spring Canyon. Or you can follow the trail above the resort ruins and climb north, then steeply east over to that same ridge.

Once atop the ridge, marred by power-line towers, descend on the unsigned but well-maintained Cold Spring Trail 1½ miles through Cold Spring Canyon—which many locals consider the prettiest in the Santa Ynez Mountains. The trail ends at Mountain Drive. You'll turn left and walk a mile along one of Santa Barbara's more bucolic byways back to your car and the Hot Springs trailhead.

[132]

28. Cold Spring Canyon

HIGHLIGHTS: Many Santa Barbarans say Cold Spring is their favorite foothill canyon. The bold rock formations and the grand views are two of a hundred good reasons for a visit.

DISTANCE: From Mountain Drive, Cold Spring Trail leads 3 miles round trip with a 900-foot elevation gain to Montecito Overlook; 7½ miles with a 2,500 gain to Montecito Peak; 9½ miles with a 2,700-foot gain to Camino Cielo.

TRANSPORTATION: From Highway 101 in Montecito, a few miles south of Santa Barbara, exit on Hot Springs Road and proceed toward the foothills for 2½ miles to Mountain Drive. Turn left. A mile's travel on Mountain Drive brings you to the Cold Spring trailhead, which begins at a point where a creek flows over a cement drainage apron.

Our favorite route to the main ridge was by a way called the Cold Spring Trail. We used to enjoy taking visitors up it, mainly because you come on the top suddenly, without warning. Then we collected remarks. Everybody, even the most stolid, said something.

—STEWART EDWARD WHITE
The Mountains, 1906

AFTER the Santa Ynez Forest Reserve was established in 1899, rangers recognized the desirability of a trail crossing the Reserve from coast to desert. A trail up the West Fork of Cold Spring Canyon had historically been the way into the Santa Barbara backcountry, but rangers realized that this tricky trail, which climbed around a waterfall and crossed shale slopes, would be difficult to maintain. In 1905, the Forest Service built a trail up the East Fork of Cold Spring Canyon.

And a lovely trail it is. It begins by the alder-shaded, year-round creek, then rises out of the canyon for fine coastal views.

THE WALK: The trail immediately crosses the creek to the east side of the canyon. It rises briefly through oak woodland, then returns to the creek. On your left, a quarter-mile from the trailhead, is the easily overlooked, unsigned West Fork Trail. This century-old trail ascends 1½ miles through California bay laurel to Gibraltar Road.

Continuing past the West Fork trail junction, the East Fork Trail rises up the canyon wall and rejoins the creek a half-mile later. Look for a fine swimming hole below you to the right. The trail then switchbacks moderately out of the canyon to Montecito Overlook. Enjoy the view of the Santa Barbara coastline and the Channel Islands.

Past the overlook, you'll cross a fire road leading down to Hot Springs Canyon, begin an uphill climb and soon encounter the Hot Springs connector trail. The one-mile-long connector trail leads down into Hot Springs Canyon. Along the trail thrive bamboo, huge agave, banana and palm trees—remnants of landscaped gardens that surrounded Hot Springs Resort during its glory days. Explore the ruins of Hot Springs Hotel, constructed during the early 1880s. Europeans and Americans from colder climes flocked here to "take the cure." A 1920 fire destroyed the hotel; it was rebuilt, but burned again in 1964.

From the junction with the Hot Springs connector trail, Cold Spring Trail switchbacks up canyon and offers fine coastal views. A one-mile climb brings you to two eucalyptus trees (about the only shade en route!) and another ¾ mile of travel takes you to the unsigned junction with a side trail leading to Montecito Peak (3,214 feet). Enjoy the view and sign the summit register.

Cold Spring Trail continues a last mile to Camino Cielo. From the Sky Road, many trails lead into the far reaches of the Santa Barbara backcountry. Enjoy the grand views and return the same way.

29. Rattlensnake Canyon

HIGHLIGHTS: Rattlesnake Canyon Trail is serpentine, but otherwise far more inviting than its name suggests. The canyon is truly a beauty and Santa Barbarans know it; the city proclaimed the canyon an offical wilderness preserve.

DISTANCE: From Skofield Park, it's a 4½ mile round trip with a 1,000-foot elevation via Rattlesnake Canyon Trail to Tin Can Meadow. To Gibraltar Road it's a 6-mile round trip with a 1,500-foot gain.

TRANSPORTATION: From downtown in Santa Barbara, go uptown (toward the mountains) on State Street to Los Olivos Street. Turn right and proceed a half-mile, passing by the Santa Barbara Mission and joining Mission Canyon Road. Follow this road past its intersection with Foothill Road and make a right on Las Canoas Road. Follow Las Canoas to Skofield Park. Leave your car on the shoulder of the road or in the large parking area near the picnic grounds. The trail begins on Las Canoas Road near the handsome stone bridge that crosses Rattlesnake Creek.

THE joys of Rattlesnake Canyon were first promoted by none other than the Santa Barbara Chamber of Commerce. Many a turn-of-the-century visitor to Santa Barbara resorts enjoyed hiking and riding in the local mountains. Eager to keep the customers satisfied, in 1902 the Chamber purchased easements from canyon homesteaders to develop a recreation trail.

"Chamber of Commerce Trail," as the Chamber called it, was an immediate success with both tourists and locals. However, to the chamber's consternation, both the trail and the canyon itself continued to be called Rattlesnake. Chamber of Commerce Canyon sounded a bit self-serving, so the chamber tried to compromise with an earlier name, Las Canoas Canyon, and adopted a 1902 resolution to

that effect. "The name of Rattlesnake Canyon is unpleasantly sugges-
tive of a reptile," it argued, "which is found no more plentifully there
than elsewhere along the mountain range and may deter some
nervous persons from visiting that most delightful locality."

In the 1960s, the city of Santa Barbara purchased the canyon as
parkland. A handsome wooden sign at the foot of the canyon proudly
proclaims: Rattlesnake Canyon Wilderness.

Red-berried toyon, manzanita with its white urn-shaped flowers,
and purple hummingbird sage cloak the slopes and offer a variety of
smells and textures. In the early spring ceanothus blooms, adding
frosty whites and blues to the gray-green thickets. Shooting stars,
larkspur, and lupine also spread their color over the slopes and
meadows.

THE WALK: From the sandstone bridge across from Skofield
Park, hike up a brief stretch of trail and join a narrow dirt road that
parallels the east side of the creek. For lovely picnicking, take any of
the steep side trails down to the creek.

The trail zigs and zags across the creek, finally continuing along the
west bank to open, grassy Tin Can Meadow. The triangular-shaped
meadow gets its name from a homesteader's cabin constructed of
chaparral framing and kerosene-can shingles and sidings. For the first
quarter of this century, Tin Can Shack was an important canyon
landmark and several guidebooks of that era mention it. It was a
popular destination for picnickers who marveled at the inspired
architecture and posed for pictures in front of it. In 1925, a brushfire
destroyed the shack and it soon disintegrated into a pile of tin.

If you're feeling energetic, hike on toward the apex of the triangular meadow where you'll find a junction. The trail bearing left takes
you ¾ mile and climbs 500 feet to its intersection with the Tunnel
Trail—and incidentally to many points of interest in the Santa Barbara backcountry. To the right, Rattlesnake Canyon Trail climbs about
three-quarters of a mile and 500 feet to its intersection with Gibraltar
Road. There you will be greeted by an unobstructed view of the South
Coast. Watch for strangely patterned triangular aircraft overhead. A
favorite hang-glider's launching peak is almost within reach.

30. Mission Creek's Seven Falls and Inspiration Point

HIGHLIGHTS: Seven Falls has been a popular destination for Santa Barbarans since before the turn of the century. The seven distinct little falls found in the bed of Mission Creek are still welcoming hikers. Even if the creek is dry, the views from Tunnel Trail and Inspiration Point are worth the ascent.

DISTANCE: From Tunnel Road to Seven Falls via Tunnel Trail and Jesusita it's a 3-mile round trip with a 400-foot elevation gain; to Inspiration Point, it's a 5-mile round trip with an 800-foot gain.

TRANSPORTATION: From the Mission, drive up Mission Canyon Road, turning right for a block on Foothill Road, then immediately turning left back onto Mission Canyon Road. At a distinct V-intersection, veer left onto Tunnel Road and drive to its end. Park along the road.

A pleasant party spent yesterday up Mission Canyon visiting noted Seven Falls and afterward eating a tempting picnic dinner in a romantic spot on the creek's bank. To reach these falls requires some active climbing, able-bodied sliding and skillful swinging. . . .

—Santa Barbara Daily Press, 1887

TUNNEL Trail was used by workers to gain access to a difficult city waterworks project launched by the city of Santa Barbara. Workmen burrowed a tunnel through the Santa Ynez Mountains to connect the watershed on the backside of the mountains to the growing little city. Braving floods, cave-ins and dangerous hydrogen gas, a crew labored eight years and finished the project in 1912.

This easy family hike in the foothills above Santa Barbara follows Tunnel Trail, joins Jesusita Trail for an exploration of the Seven Falls along Mission Creek and ascends Inspiration Point for sweeping coastal views.

Mission Creek provided the water supply for Mission Santa Barbara. Near the Mission, which you'll pass as you proceed to Tunnel trailhead, are some stone remains of the padres' waterworks system. Mission Creek also flows through the Santa Barbara Botanic Garden, which is well worth visiting because of its fine displays of native California flora. Paths lead through chaparral, coastal sage and succulent environments to a Mission Creek dam built by the Spanish friars and Indian laborers.

A ramble through the Santa Barbara foothills combined with a visit to the Mission and Botanic Garden would add up to a very pleasant day's outing.

THE WALK: From the end of Tunnel Road, hike past a locked gate onto a paved road, which soon turns to dirt as you leave the power lines behind and get increasingly grander views of Santa Barbara. The road makes a sharp left and crosses a bridge over the West Fork of Mission Creek.

Beyond the bridge, you'll hike a short distance under some handsome oaks to a junction. (Tunnel Trail angles northeast, uphill, leading three miles to "the sky road," East Camino Cielo.) You join Jesusita Trail and descend briefly, but steeply, to Mission Creek.

At the canyon bottom, you can hike up-creek into a steep gorge that was cut from solid sandstone. Geologically inclined hikers will recognize fossilized layers of oyster beds from the Oligocene Epoch, deposited some 35 million years ago. In more recent times, say for the last few thousands of winters, rainwater has rushed from the shoulder of La Cumbre Peak and cut away at the sandstone layers, forming several deep pools. If you decide to hike up Mission Creek, be careful; reaching the waterfalls—particularly the higher ones—requires quite a bit of boulder-hopping and rock-climbing. Even when there's not much water in the creek, it can be tricky going.

From the creek crossing, Jesusita Trail switchbacks steeply up the chaparral-cloaked canyon wall to a power line road atop a knoll.

[138]

Although Inspiration Point is not all that inspiring, the view from the cluster of sandstone rocks at the 1,750-foot viewpoint is worth the climb. You can see the coastline quite some distance north and south, as well as Catalina and the Channel Islands, Santa Barbara and the Goleta Valley.

31. Knapp's Castle

HIGHLIGHTS: Picturesque ruins of George Owen Knapp's vacation home in top-of-the-world setting. Great ocean, island and backcountry views.

DISTANCE: From Paradise Road to Knapp's Castle via Snyder Trail it's 6½ miles round trip with a 2,000-foot elevation gain. Knapp's Castle the easy way from Camino Cielo is a one mile round trip.

TRANSPORTATION: From Highway 101 in Santa Barbara, exit on Highway 154 and proceed 8 miles to East Camino Cielo. Turn right and drive 2½ miles to a saddle, where you'll spot a parking area and a locked Forest Service gate.

Directions to Paradise Road trailhead: From Highway 101 in Santa Barbara, exit on Highway 154 and proceed 11½ miles up and over San Marcos Pass to Paradise Road. Turn right and proceed 4.4 miles to a turnout on the right side of the road. (If you spot the road leading to Sage Hill Campground, you went a little too far on Paradise Road.) The trail begins at a dirt road that's closed to vehicles.

This tract, at the edge of the grand canyon of the Santa Ynez Mountains, is one of the most magnificent, in point of scenic glories, in California.

—the view from Knapp's Castle, as reported
by the *Santa Barbara Morning Press,* April 9, 1916

IN 1916, George Owen Knapp's recurrent bouts of hay fever sent him high into the Santa Ynez Mountains behind Santa Barbara to seek relief. The wealthy former chairman of the board of Union Carbide found relief—and an ideal locale to build the mountain home of his dreams.

The high, huge, and presumably hypo-allergenic parcel belonged to Homer Snyder, once the chef at Santa Barbara's Arlington Hotel. Back in 1902, Snyder had built a rustic hostelry atop Camino Cielo, "the sky road." Visitors during the early 1900s included Theodore Roosevelt and William Howard Taft. Knapp bought the Snyder place, renamed it Laurel Springs Ranch, and charitably offered it as a weekend retreat for Santa Barbara's hardworking nurses and hospital workers.

Knapp's dream home, carved from thick sandstone blocks, took four years to complete. It was a magnificent residence, complete with illuminated waterfalls and a room housing one of Knapp's other passions—a huge pipe organ.

While Knapp was developing his private retreat, he was also helping to boost public access to the Santa Barbara Forest Reserve, as it was known in those days. Knapp and a couple of his wealthy friends were tireless promoters of roads and trails, in order to make the backcountry accessible to all. Knapp's enthusiasm and money helped extend trails west to the top of Refugio Canyon (now part-time rancher Ronald Reagan's spread) and east to Ojai.

The trail-building efforts of Knapp and his buddies were much appreciated by the local populace. As a 1917 editorial in the *Santa Barbara Daily News* put it: "They are strong advocates of the great out-of-doors, and under their leadership places in the wild heretofore denied humans because of utter inaccessibility are being opened up to the hiker and horseback rider."

Knapp was sixty-something when he threw himself into his castle-building and trail-building efforts. He spent most of the rest of his long, productive life in his castle in the sky. In 1940, he sold his retreat to Frances Holden, who nearly became the first and only person to lose money in the Santa Barbara real estate market when a forest fire destroyed the castle just five months after she bought it. Fortunately, she had insurance.

Stone walls, part of the foundation, and a couple of chimneys are all that remain of Knapp's Castle. But the view of the Santa Barbara backcountry is still magnificent, particularly if you arrive at sunset and watch the purple shadows skim over the Santa Ynez and San Rafael Mountains.

Snyder Trail, which receives sporadic maintenance from the Santa Barbara Sierra Club and the U.S. Forest Service, leads to the castle ruins. The upper part of the trail, formerly Knapp's long driveway to his retreat, offers an easy walk down to the ruins from Camino Cielo. From Paradise Road, Snyder Trail takes you on a steep ascent to the castle. Quite an aerobic workout, if you're in the mood.

THE WALK (from Paradise Road): From the turnout, walk 50 yards up the dirt road to the signed beginning of the Snyder Trail, which is actually the road you're following. The road passes under some stately oaks and after a quarter-mile reaches a large green water tank.

The road narrows to a trail, passes some planted pines and a second water tank, then begins ascending a series of switchbacks. For the most part, you'll be climbing in shade. Behind and below are good views of the canyon cut by the Santa Ynez River.

About two miles from the trailhead, Snyder Trail joins an abandoned dirt road. The old road/trail crosses a cottonwood-lined seasonal creek and tunnels beneath the boughs of pungent bay laurel. Around a bend you'll get your first glimpse of Knapp's Castle, then ascend another three-quarter mile to the ruins.

THE WALK (from Camino Cielo): It's a short half-mile descent on dirt road to the castle. Chamise, ceanothus, toyon and other members of the hardy chaparral family line the old road.

From the ruins of Knapp's Castle, enjoy the view of the Santa Ynez River, Cachuma Lake and the wide blue Pacific. And take in the panorama of peaks from Mount Pinos to Figueroa Mountain to the Casmalia Hills.

32. Aliso Canyon Nature Trail

HIGHLIGHTS: A great introduction to the Santa Barbara Backcountry is Aliso Canyon Nature Trail in the Santa Ynez Recreation Area of Los Padres National Forest. The loop trail follows Aliso Creek and climbs to a ridgetop viewpoint. A brochure describing the natural attractions found along the trail is available at the trailhead and at a nearby ranger station. Because of its importance, the nature trail earned the federal "National Recreation Trail" designation.

DISTANCE: Aliso Canyon Nature Trail is a 3-mile loop with a 500-foot elevation gain.

TRANSPORTATION: From Highway 101 in Santa Barbara, take the Lake Cachuma/Highway 154 exit. Follow 154 as it ascends into the Santa Ynez Mountains. At San Marcos Pass, the road crests. A short distance over the pass, just past a Vista Point (about 10 miles from Santa Barbara if you're watching your odometer), turn right on Paradise Road and drive 4 miles to the signed turnoff on your left for Los Prietos Ranger Station and Sage Hill Campground. (You can pick up a brochure keyed to Aliso Canyon Nature Trail, as well as books and maps, at the ranger station). Follow the winding road a short distance across the Santa Ynez River and through Sage Hill Campground to the signed trailhead.

IN a relatively short distance, Aliso Canyon Nature Trail explores a variety of typical backcountry plant communities—oak woodland, grassland and chaparral. The canyon takes its name from white and gray-barked sycamores *(alisos)* that grow in the canyon.

Even during drought periods when the Santa Ynez River is bone-dry, Aliso Canyon is usually green. And the spring wildflower display, while far from spectacular, isn't half-bad. Purple lupine, golden California poppies and red Indian paintbrush color the canyon.

THE WALK: The trail heads north along the bottom of Aliso Canyon, which is filled with coast live oak and sycamore. You'll soon pass the signed junction with Upper Oso Trail, which comes in from the right; this will be your return route.

After a mile, the path leaves Aliso Canyon, zigzags east up a steep shale slope, then skirts a lovely meadow. Blue-eyed grass, popcorn flower and California poppies dot the meadow. In the meadowland, you'll find a signed junction. One trail heads straight ahead (east) to Upper Oso Camp and a junction with Santa Cruz Trail. This trail presents a great opportunity to extend your hike. A mile and half of travel along Santa Cruz Trail brings you to Nineteen Oaks Camp and four miles of trekking to Little Pine Mountain.

Aliso Canyon Trail turns right (south) at the junction and switchbacks up a hill to the high point of the nature trail. You'll enjoy good views of the Santa Ynez Mountains to the south, the San Rafael Mountains to the north.

The trail descends a morning glory- and sage-covered slope to the lip of Santa Ynez Canyon, sculpted long-ago by the erosive action of the Santa Ynez River. You get a good view of the river far below. During dry years, the river sometimes doesn't look like much—just a few shallow pools—but it's actually the longest stretch of free-flowing river in Southern California.

The trail travels along a precipice for a short time, then switchbacks down to the bottom of Aliso Canyon. Near the canyon mouth, you'll intersect the path where you started, head left, and soon return to the trailhead.

Western Sycamore

California Poppy

33. Little Pine Mountain

HIGHLIGHTS: Santa Cruz Trail presents a lengthy climb, but rewards the hiker with a superb view of the Channel Islands and the Pacific. The trail tops Little Pine Mountain, an ecological island of conifers that one might expect to find only in the High Sierra. Another destination, ponderosa pine-shaded Happy Hollow Camp, is appropriately named.
DISTANCE: Following Santa Cruz Trail from Upper Oso Camp to Nineteen Oaks Camp is a 3½-mile round trip with a 600-foot elevation gain; to Little Pine Saddle, a 10-mile round trip with a 3,300-foot gain; to Happy Hollow Camp, a 13-mile round trip with a 3,300-foot gain.
TRANSPORTATION: From U.S. 101 in Santa Barbara, exit on California 154 and proceed northwest 11 miles over San Marcos Pass. Turn right onto Paradise Road and follow it east for 6 miles along the Santa Ynez River. Just after crossing the river and passing through a parking area, turn left on Oso Road and follow it a mile to Upper Oso Campground. Hiker parking is provided at the eastern end of the camp at the trailhead.

HIKERS can work up quite a sweat while ascending the hot, exposed slope of Little Pine Mountain. Start trekking in the cool of the morning when the trail is shadowed and enjoy your lunch at the top beneath the boughs of a big cone spruce. An ocean breeze usually keeps the mountaintop cool.

Families with young children may enjoy the easy part of Santa Cruz Trail—the first stretch leading to the quiet pools of Oso Creek and to picnicking at Nineteen Oaks Camp. Hikers in good condition or those looking for a good conditioning hike will relish the challenge of the climb to the top of Little Pine Mountain.

THE WALK: The trek begins at a locked gate beyond the campground and for the first mile follows Camuesa Fire Road which, unfortunately, is a Forest Service designated "motorcycle route." The road stays just to the east of Oso Creek, where there are several fine swimming pools. When the road takes a sharp hairpin turn, hikers leave the two- and three-wheeled locusts behind by continuing straight ahead at a signed junction and joining Santa Cruz Trail.

For the next mile the trail is relatively flat, although it drops in and out of washes on the east side of Oso Creek. Soon the hiker sees a signed spur trail on the right, which leads one-tenth mile to Nineteen Oaks Camp. Oaks shade this camp, but not 19 of them.

Santa Cruz Trail heads north, crosses Oso Creek, and begins switchbacking through grassy meadows. Dipping in and out of brush-smothered canyons, you ascend a hill to a saddle between the ridge you're traveling and Little Pine Mountain.

The trail soon switchbacks north, then west across the south face of Little Pine Mountain. You'll cross two large meadows, called "Mellow Meadows" by laid-back Santa Barbarans. The tall dry grass is the habitat of deer and even an occasional mountain lion. The trail climbs around the heads of a half-dozen canyons before reaching Alexander Saddle. To the left, a bulldozed road goes to 4,107-foot Alexander Peak. Santa Cruz Trail continues straight. You bear right on the connector trail that leads to Happy Hollow Camp.

From Alexander Saddle, the connector trail climbs steeply at first up the dramatic Little Pine Mountain ridgeline. Weatherworn pines on the ridge offer shade and you'll catch fabulous views of the Channel Islands, Santa Ynez Valley, and Lake Cachuma. Large sugar pines and a few live oaks cling to the north face of Little Pine Peak. Farther along the trail you will be among yellow pine, spruce, and Douglas fir. The top of Little Pine Mountain is a great place to unpack your lunch or take a snooze.

From the peak, the trail descends a short way to Happy Hollow Camp, nestled among ponderosa pine, fir and oak. The camp has a few tables and stoves. During the 1930s, this camp was a recreation site for Civilian Conservation Corps workmen. The name Happy Hollow is apt; the camp is indeed in a hollow, and hikers are no doubt happy after a 3,300-foot elevation gain in 6 miles.

34. Santa Ynez River

HIGHLIGHTS: The California State Water Resources Control Board suggests that one of the most beneficial uses of the upper Santa Ynez River is for "water contact recreation." Translated from bureaucratic jargon: "Go jump in the river!" Except for years of scant rainfall, great swimming holes await hikers who venture to the attractive Santa Ynez Recreation Area, located in the mountains behind Santa Barbara.
DISTANCE: From Red Rock trailhead to Gibraltar Dam Picnic Area via river trail is 6 miles round trip; 400-foot elevation gain.
TRANSPORTATION: From Highway 101 in Santa Barbara, take the "Lake Cachuma, Highway 154" exit. Proceed east on Highway 154. At the top of San Marcos Pass, you'll spot the historic Cielo Store, featured as "Papadakis Tavern," in the remake of "The Postman Always Rings Twice." A short distance over the pass, just past a Vista Point (about 10 miles from Santa Barbara if you're watching your odometer), turn right on Paradise Road and drive to the end of the road—10.7 miles. Leave your car in the large dirt parking lot adjacent to the trail, which begins at a locked gate.

DURING dry years, the river's swimming holes are filled by periodic releases from Gibraltar Reservoir, located up-river from the recreation area. Thanks to Santa Barbara's contribution of a small part of its municipal water supply, some of the pools maintain year-round depths of 6 to 18 feet.

Santa Ynez River Trail leads to several pleasant swimming holes and is an easy hike, suitable for the whole family. The most popular ol' swimmin' hole is Red Rock Pool, located only a short distance from the trailhead. The trail to the pools and to Gibraltar Dam Picnic Area follows the remains of an old mining road, built in the 1870s during a quicksilver mining boom. The road was later used by workers during the 1920 construction of Gibraltar Dam.

For more information about the Santa Ynez Recreation Area, stop by Los Padres National Forest Los Prietos Ranger Station, located about midway between Highway 154 and Red Rock Trailhead on Paradise Road.

If you're the kind of hiker who loves loop trips, note the presence of a second trail leading from the parking lot to Gibraltar Dam. The "high road," as it's known by locals, makes a gentle traverse across the mountains above the river. Like the "low road"—Santa Ynez River Trail—it's about three miles long. It's a good trail to keep in mind for times of high water.

THE WALK: Wide, flat Santa Ynez River Trail passes a "No Nudity Allowed" sign, and after a quarter-mile, crosses the river. Near this crossing you might observe some scattered bricks, all that remains of a turn-of-the-century quicksilver furnace. Quicksilver ore, mined in the nearby hills, was crushed and heated in the furnace. The ore became gaseous at a low temperature and the gas condensed into liquid mercury. Mercury, a very heavy element, was transported in small, foot-long cylinders, each weighing about 75 pounds.

Soon after the first river crossing, you'll reach Red Rock, the most popular swimming hole. Geologically minded hikers will examine the red rock, metamorphosed volcanics of the Jurassic age. Other hikers will plunge into the river.

The trail passes through oak woodland and zigzags from bank to bank along the river. Alongside the river is a canopy of cottonwood, sycamore and willow.

Wildlife-viewing opportunities, particularly during the early morning hours, are quite good near the Santa Ynez River because the area includes several different habitats: oak woodland, coastal sage scrub, grassland and freshwater marsh. You might spot a deer, gray fox, striped skunk, lizard, cottontail rabbit or raccoon. Watch for pond turtles basking on the rocks, logs and banks of large pools.

The ecological diversity of the area also means a wide variety of birdlife. In the woodland areas, birders might sight a mourning dove, warbling vireo, northern oriole or a woodpecker. Cliff swallows, fly-catchers and belted kingfishers swoop over the river.

Several more dry river crossings and a couple of wet ones, and some travel beneath the boughs of some handsome coast live oaks, will bring you to Gibraltar Picnic Area, located a few hundred yards down-river from the dam. Oaks shade some picnic tables.

You may continue up the trail to Gibraltar Dam, named for the large rock here, which is said to resemble the great guardian rock of the Mediterranean. A second, shadeless picnic site is located at the southeast top edge of the dam. Observe the warning signs at the dam and stay out of restricted areas.

35. Above Lake Cachuma on Tequepis Trail

HIGHLIGHTS: Cachuma Lake, besides storing an important part of Santa Barbara County's water supply, is a popular weekend destination for Southland anglers, campers and bird-watchers. For the hiker, Tequepis Trail offers the best view of the lake, as well as a 360-degree panorama from the high peaks of Los Padres National Forest to the Channel Islands. It's one of the most beautiful, yet least-used, trails in the Santa Ynez Mountains.

DISTANCE: From Camp Cielo to West Camino Cielo via Tequepis Trail is 8 miles round trip with a 2,300-foot elevation gain; to Broadcast Peak, 9 miles round trip with a 2,800-foot gain.

TRANSPORTATION: From Highway 101 in Santa Barbara, exit on Highway 154 (San Marcos Pass Road) and drive 17½ miles to a left turn lane and a road leading left signed "Cachuma Camp" and "Camp Cielo." Proceed with caution over the first half of this road, which is dirt and full of potholes. The second half of the 1.3-mile road is paved. Park in a dirt lot just outside the wooden gate of the Campfire Girls' Camp Cielo. Walk, don't drive, up the asphalt service road into the camp.

MUCH of Tequepis Trail is shaded with live oak and sycamore. Near the top, are two arboreal surprises—tan oak and madrone, trees more commonly found in the northern part of the state. In springtime, lupine, bush poppy and other wildflowers splash color along the trail.

Tequepis, possibly the most carefully pronounced trail name in Southern California, is the Chumash word for seed-gatherer. Indians beat the grasses on nearby slopes with a tennis racket-like tool to gather the seeds.

You can get an eagle's-eye-view of Cachuma Lake by taking Tequepis Trail and you can get an eagle's-eye-view of eagles on a two-hour boat cruise. More than 100 bald eagles make the shores of Cachuma their winter home. Eagle Tours, conducted by the park's naturalist, offer a close-up look at the eagles, as well as dozens of other resident and migratory birds.

THE WALK: Hike up the paved camp road 75 yards, past a swimming pool, to the signed beginning of the trail. Tequepis Trail, actually the camp road for its first quarter-mile, passes some tiny A-frame tent cabins. Leaving "Magic Forest Camp" behind, the dirt road crosses and recrosses a seasonal creek. Only after a good winter rain is there water in the creek.

You'll ignore a side road to the right and a bulldozer track to your left and arrive face-to-face with what appears to be a gigantic Egyptian shroud pin. The hieroglyphics on it read: Seaboard Ohio, Santa Ynez Unit #2. There's a water pipeline below ground.

One mile from the trailhead, the dirt road dead-ends. Signed Tequepis Trail, from this point forward a narrow path, veers left. The trail climbs moderately for a quarter-mile, then very steeply for another quarter-mile. After this strenuous stretch, the path ascends at a more accommodating pace via well-graded switchbacks.

About a mile from the top, you'll get a great view of the lake, then pass near a stand of cinnamon-colored madrone. In bloom, the small tree sprouts white urn-shaped flowers and clusters of red-orange berries. Farther along the trail, look for the tan oak, or tanbark oak, a handsome tree more often associated with redwood or Douglas fir forest.

The trail tops a ridge and ends at unpaved West Camino Cielo. From the ridgetop just above the road, you'll have commanding views to the north of the San Rafael and Sierra Madre Mountains. Just below is Cachuma Lake and the Santa Ynez Valley. Far to the east you might spot Mount Pinos, highest peak in Los Padres National Forest. To the south is a good view of Isla Vista and the University of California at Santa Barbara, and the state beaches of Refugio and El Capitan. Anacapa, Santa Cruz, Santa Rosa and San Miguel islands float upon the horizon. If looking south to view the ocean is a bit disconcerting, remember that both Santa Barbara County's coastline, and the Santa Ynez Mountains that parallel it, stretch from east to west.

If you're still feeling frisky and want to do a little bushwhacking, take the very rough and steep side trail from the ridgetop to Broadcast Peak. Thrash a half-mile through manzanita and yerba santa up to the 4,028-foot summit, which is crowned with the transmitting tower of Santa Barbara television station KEYT. The peak and its great views can also be reached by West Camino Cielo, a longer but much easier route. Ultra-energetic hikers can continue another mile west on West Camino Cielo to the lookout on 4,298-foot Santa Ynez Peak.

36. Zaca Lake

HIGHLIGHTS: Long ago, the Chumash called the lake *Zaca* or "quiet place." The name still fits today. Zaca Lake, a private enclave within the boundaries of Los Padres National Forest, is a secluded spot offering canoeing, swimming and hiking.

DISTANCE: To Cedros Saddle via Sulphur Spring Trail is a 4½-mile round trip with a 1,000-foot elevation gain. Looping back to the trailhead via Zaca Ridge Road is a 6½ mile round trip with 1,500-foot gain. Shorter and longer hikes are possible.

TRANSPORTATION: From Highway 101, some 50 miles up-coast from Santa Barbara, exit on Zaca Station Road. (This exit is first one past 101's junction with Highway 154.) You'll drive 3¼ miles, passing vineyards and the Firestone Winery, to a junction with Foxen Canyon Road. Bear left, heading north 3½ miles to the poorly signed turnoff for Zaca Lake. Turn right onto the road leading to the lake. It's paved for the first mile or so, dirt for the next five. Take your time and watch for potholes. Sign in at the lodge and pay the day-use fee.

From the lodge, drive down the dirt road another half-mile to the picnic ground. Park in the shade.

Zaca Lake hours are 8 a.m. to dusk daily. Day use fees are adults $5, children 13 and younger $3, dogs $3. Because the lake and lodge is occasionally rented to private parties, it's a good idea to call the Human Potential Foundation at Zaca Lake Lodge, (805) 688-4819, before you set out for a hike.

ZACA is one of the very few natural lakes in Southern California. The lake is replenished by underground springs (a somewhat rare occurrence), so it doesn't suffer to the degree that the usual rain-fed lakes do during the Southland's long droughts.

Geologists speculate that Zaca Lake was formed about 10,000 years ago by a landslide. Before this slide, underground springs fed Zaca

Creek, which meandered through Zaca Canyon. But loosened by fault activity and heavy rains, one of Zaca Canyon's walls collapsed, forming a dam across the canyon. This natural dam has contained rain run-off and underground sources within the boundaries of a small lake ever since.

The Chumash, the native Americans who inhabited this area for thousands of years before the white man came, had a different explanation for the formation of Zaca Lake: One day, an arrogant man was walking around the Zaca Canyon area when he looked up and saw Thunder. The unthinking man spoke insultingly to this mighty being. His fellow villagers were appalled by this disrespect and fled the scene. Thunder, enraged at the man who offended him, sat down on the village, squashing the insolent fellow and making a great hole in the earth which became Zaca Lake.

Zaca Lake has a colorful history. During the 1890s, a Frenchman, John Baptiste Libeu, was the caretaker of the lake and surrounding ranchland for his boss, owner James Westley Calkins. One day a government surveyor came along and announced to Libeu that the lake and surrounding land did not belong to Calkins, but to the federal government. Libeu promptly rode into the land office in Santa Barbara and filed a homestead claim on the land—much to Calkin's displeasure.

Libeu and his family operated a small hostelry for overnight guests. The lake was a particularly popular locale for silent moviemakers from Santa Barbara's Flying A Studios. Although Flying A in 1913 had the largest, most up-to-date film studio in the world, its filmmakers often went on location. Zaca Lake and environs were featured in many serials, melodramas and westerns.

In those innocent years when conflict-of-interest questions were rarely raised, Libeu also worked for the government. He was the forest ranger for the Pine Mountain and Zaca Lake Reserve, set aside in 1898. Libeu enforced hunting, homestead and fire regulations for the reserve, later named the Santa Barbara Forest Reserve (and still later Los Padres National Forest). At one time Libeu was the district ranger in charge of an immense territory stretching from the Santa Ynez River to the Cuyama River, from near Santa Maria to the Ventura County line.

Today Zaca Lake is owned by the Human Potential Foundation "dedicated to the expansion of human awareness." The Foundation's facilities are rented out to New Age and community service groups, as well as to the traveling public. There's also a campground by the lake.

Several trails explore the Los Padres National Forest backcountry above Zaca Lake. Not all of them are in good shape, however, so it's best to ask at the lodge before you hit the trail.

THE WALK: From the picnic ground, walk up the dirt road a half-mile to the signed beginning of Sulphur Spring Trail. Note another, unsigned trail, on your right; this very steep trail is your return route.

Sulphur Spring Trail ascends sometimes moderately, sometimes steeply, a bit under two miles to Cedros Saddle and an intersection with dirt Zaca Ridge Road. Just below the saddle is a grove of incense cedar. The cedar, along with various kinds of pines, were planted on the ridges around Zaca Lake during various forest service projects beginning about 1910. The incense cedar in these parts are doing well, but some trees—the Monterey pine for example—fared poorly in this part of the national forest.

(Sulphur Spring Trail resumes on the other side of Zaca Ridge Road and descends steeply to the northeast to Manzana Creek on the edge of the San Rafael Wilderness. For a grand view of the wilderness, the Sierra Madre Mountains and Hurricane Deck, walk a hundred yards down the trail.)

This hike heads right on Zaca Ridge Road, climbing moderately to a junction with Zaca Peak Road. You'll bear right (west on this dirt road) and continue a mile to an orange flag, which marks the very steeply descending trail that will complete the loop back to the trailhead.

Ambitious hikers can continue west on Zaca Peak Road toward prominent Zaca Peak. Although the road passes below the peak (which is extremely difficult to reach because of the thick brush and bad trail), you can get a pretty good view right from the road. At the turn of the century, the first fire lookout station in what was to become Los Padres National Forest was established atop the peak.

Ultra-ambitious hikers can continue several more miles past Zaca Peak to well-named Lookout Mountain.

[155]

37. Figueroa Mountain's Fascinating Flora

HIGHLIGHTS: One of the best ways to explore Figueroa Mountain, surely one of the most botanically intriguing peaks in Southern California, is via La Jolla Trail. During good wildflower years, you'll get Sound of Music-style vistas of—and from—the mountain. During mediocre wildflower years you can still enjoy the mountain's tall trees, bubbling stream, fine trails. Figueroa Mountain Recreation Area is one of the prettiest and most pleasant places in Los Padres National Forest.
DISTANCE: From Figueroa Mountain Road to Ballard Trail Camp via La Jolla Trail it's a 4-mile round trip with a 1,100-foot elevation gain.
TRANSPORTATION: From Highway 101, about 6 miles north of Solvang, exit on Highway 154 and head 5 miles to Figueroa Mountain Road and turn left. Wind about 12 miles (½-mile past Figueroa Ranger Station) to its intersection with dirt Tunnell Road coming in from the right. Park in the small dirt lot.

FIGUEROA Mountain's upper slopes are forested with yellow pine, Coulter pine and big cone spruce. The yellow pine is a tall regal tree with a reddish bark that looks fashioned of rectangular mosaic tiles. It's a three-needled pine, as is the Coulter, which produces huge cones, the largest and heaviest of our native conifers. Tree-lovers will find plenty of other arboreal companions, including large specimens of California bay laurel and big leaf maple, and picturesque coastal, valley and blue oaks.

Spring wildflower displays on lower slopes are often good, sometimes exceptional. Among the more common roadside and trailside flowers are fiddleneck, Johnny jump-ups, shooting stars, lupine and cream cups.

La Jolla Trail (Trail 30W10 on Los Padres National Forest map) received its name from dependable La Jolla Spring located near Ballard Trail Camp, a tranquil retreat on the banks of Birabent Creek. William Ballard was in charge of the Wells Fargo Stage Depot in the Santa Ynez Valley during the 1880s. He liked to hunt and fish and often camped in the area where the Forest Service's tiny trail camp is now located. After working up an appetite on the hike to Ballard Camp, you might want to drop in at a later Santa Ynez Valley stage stop, now a restaurant—historic Mattei's Tavern in Los Olivos.

La Jolla Trail is an "upside down" trail; that is, the descent—moderate to steep—occurs during the first half of the hike. Pace yourself accordingly.

From Ballard Camp, the hiker can saunter down Birabent Creek a half-mile or so to an abandoned trail camp once known as Lower Ballard Camp.

THE WALK: La Jolla Trail begins in a saddle once known as Sawmill Basin. Harvey Stonebarger bought timber rights from the Forest Service during the years 1914-17 and constructed a sawmill here. The timber proved to be of poor quality and he soon removed his sawmill.

La Jolla Trail descends northwest through a mountain meadow fringed with blue oaks and seasonally bedecked with goldfields and lupine. As you lose elevation, you pass through a mixed oak-and-pine woodland, then head down the north side of a small canyon watered by seasonal Ballard Creek. Once out of the woods, the flower show (nature willing) begins again on a slope dotted with clarkias, California poppies, phacelias, Plummer's mariposa lillies and Chinese houses.

More switchbacks and descending bring you to creekside Ballard Trail Camp, shaded by towering oaks and sycamores. If you saunter down-creek a ways you'll discover the crumpled remains of an old pump station once used by oil workers to bring water to their drill sites high above the creek.

Return the same way.

38. Fir Canyon and Figueroa Mountain via Davy Brown Trail

HIGHLIGHTS: Figueroa Mountain, located in Los Padres National Forest 25 air miles behind Santa Barbara, is one of the most botanically diverse areas in Southern California. A great way to explore the mountain's flora and colorful history is to hike Davy Brown Trail, which ascends cool, moist Fir Canyon, climbs to the headwaters of Davy Brown Creek and visits the Forest Service fire lookout atop 4,528-foot Figueroa Mountain. Great views!

DISTANCE: From Davy Brown Camp via Davy Brown Trail to Harry Roberts Cabin is 3½ miles round trip with a 900-foot elevation gain; to Figueroa Mt. Rd. 6¼ miles round trip with a 1,700-foot gain; to Figueroa Mt. Lookout 7½ miles round trip with a 2,400-foot gain.

TRANSPORTATION: From Highway 101 in Santa Barbara, exit on Highway 154 and proceed 14 miles over Cachuma Pass and past Lake Cachuma to Armour Ranch Road. Turn right and drive 1.3 miles to Happy Canyon Road. Make a right and wind 14 pleasant miles to Cachuma Saddle Station. To reach the lower Davy Brown trailhead, you'll bear right at the saddle onto Sunset Valley Road and proceed 5 miles to Davy Brown Campground. To reach upper Davy Brown trailhead, bear left at Cachuma Saddle Station onto Figueroa Mountain Road and drive 5 miles to a turnout and signed Davy Brown Trail on your right.

You can also gain access to both trailheads by exiting Highway 101 north of the Buellton turnoff on Highway 154, turning left on Figueroa Mountain Road and driving 15 miles to the upper trailhead. During wildflower season consider a drive up Figueroa Mountain Road and down Happy Canyon Road—or vice-versa—to make a scenic loop through the Santa Barbara Backcountry.

FIGUEROA Mountain's upper slopes are forested with Coulter pine, yellow pine and big cone spruce. Spring wildflower displays on the lower slopes are often exceptional. Among the more common roadside and trailside flowers are fiddleneck, Johnny jump-ups, shooting stars, lupine and cream cups.

At lower elevations are abundant digger pine. Its distinguishing features are long needles in bunches of three and the forking broom-like appearance of its trunk. The pines are named for a tribe of Indians in California's gold country, who were disparagingly called "diggers" by the '49ers.

On higher slopes grow other three-needled pines—the yellow pine and the Coulter pine, which produces huge cones, the largest and heaviest of any native conifer. The mountain honors Jose Figueroa, Mexican governor of California from 1833 to 1835. Anyone who climbs to the mountain's lookout, where there are grand views of the San Rafael Wilderness, Santa Ynez Valley, Point Conception and the Channel Islands, will agree that having such a mountain take your name is indeed an honor.

THE WALK: From the northwest end of Davy Brown Camp, you'll pass a green gate and a vehicle barrier and join the unsigned trail. You'll head west through forested Munch Canyon, cross Davy Brown Creek a couple of times, then begin angling southwest up Fir Canyon. Actually, no firs grow in Fir Canyon but its southern cousin, the big cone spruce, is plentiful here.

About 1¾ miles from the trailhead, you'll descend into a blue oak-shaded draw and arrive at the ruins of chrome miner Harry Robert's cabin, built in the 1920s. A large big leaf maple shades the cabin, which is a good lunch stop or turnaround point if you're not feeling too energetic.

Beyond the cabin, maple-shaded Davy Brown Trail crosses and recrosses the creek. Keep a sharp lookout right for the unsigned side trail leading to Figueroa Mountain Lookout. (If you see signed Munch Canyon Spur Trail on your left, you overshot the trail; double back a hundred yards.)

Those wishing to follow Davy Brown Trail to its end will continue ascending along Davy Brown Creek through a wet world of mushrooms and banana slugs under the shade of oaks and laurel. A half-mile from the top of the trail you'll step carefully over a splintered white Monterey shale outcropping at a point where the canyon makes a sharp turn. Old-timers called this bend the Devil's Elbow.

Davy Brown Trail climbs to the headwaters of Davy Brown Creek, then out onto a grassy slope dotted with digger pine and buttercups. You might encounter a herd of bovine forest-users on this grassy slope. Trail's end is Figueroa Mountain Road.

Figueroa Mountain Lookout-bound hikers will head right at the above-mentioned junction. The path gains elevation rapidly as it climbs out onto a drier slope cloaked in chaparral—toyon, ceanothus, black sage, scrub oak and mountain mahogany.

The trail descends for a short distance to a tiny meadow then immediately climbs steeply again. As the trail nears the top, notice the progression of pines from digger to Coulter to yellow.

The trail intersects a road to Figueroa Peak. Bear left on the road a half-mile to the lookout. Enjoy the far-reaching views of the major peaks of Los Padres National Forest and of the coast and Channel Islands.

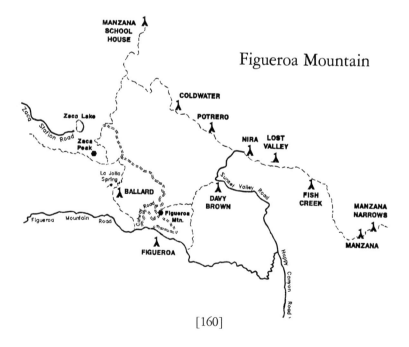

Figueroa Mountain

39. Up Manzana Creek to Manzana Narrows

HIGHLIGHTS: Manzana Creek Trail passes tall thin alders and in spring, wildflowers. Four creekside camps beckon the picnicker. In addition to a few stocked trout that survive the legions of fishermen, you'll find frogs, crayfish and turtles in Manzana Creek. Rewarding the hiker after many stream crossings is Manzana Narrows, a narrow part of the canyon where there are some fine pools for fishing and cooling-off.
DISTANCE: From NIRA to Lost Valley Camp via Manzana Creek Trail it's 2 miles round trip with a 100-foot elevation gain; to Fish Creek Camp it's 6 miles round trip with a 400-foot gain; to Manzana Camp it's 12 miles round trip with 1,100-foot gain; to Manzana Narrows it's 14 miles round trip with a 1,200-foot gain.
TRANSPORTATION: From U.S. 101 in Santa Barbara, exit on California 154 and follow the latter highway over San Marcos Pass. Beyond Lake Cachuma, turn right on Armour Ranch Road and proceed 2½ miles to Happy Canyon Road. Make another right and continue 17 miles (Happy Canyon Road becomes Sunset Valley Road after passing an intersection at Figueroa Mountain Road) to NIRA Camp. Parking space for hikers is provided at the south end of the campground.

SAN Rafael Wilderness was the first Wilderness Area set aside under the Federal Wilderness Act of 1964.

"San Rafael is rocky, rugged, wooded and lonely," President Lyndon B. Johnson remarked when he signed the San Rafael Wilderness bill on March 21, 1968. "I believe it will enrich the spirit of America."

Manzana Creek Trail begins at NIRA, the major entry point for the San Rafael Wilderness. NIRA, an auto camp and popular day use area, is an acronym for the National Industrial Recovery Act, a Federal program launched during the Depression.

THE WALK: Leaving NIRA Camp the trail immediately crosses Manzana Creek and begins a gentle ascent along the north bank of the creek. The route switchbacks up a low ridge cloaked with digger pine, and soon arrives at Lost Valley Camp, a small site tucked among oak and pine at the mouth of Lost Valley Canyon. This canyon reaches from Manzana Creek up to Hurricane Deck, heart of the San Rafael Wilderness. Lost Valley Trail departs from camp and climbs up to the magnificent deck.

Manzana Creek Trail meanders along the north bank of the creek for the next two miles. Look to your right across the creek and you'll spot Fish Creek Camp on the far side of the Manzana floodplain, where Fish Creek meets Manzana Creek. Fishermen like this camp because the creeks here usually support a large trout population.

Past Fish Creek, Manzana Creek Trail at first stays on the north wall of the canyon, passing through chaparral, and dipping in and out of washes. Manzana Canyon narrows and the trail heads down toward the creek, which is lined by tall thin alders. The trail crosses the Manzana, and a half-mile later, crosses again. The canyon narrows even more and, after a few more creek crossings, the path brings you to Manzana Camp. Located beneath picturesque live oak, the camp offers a dependable water supply, fishing and swimming pools. The manzanita, which gave its name to half the geographical features around here, abounds.

Beyond this camp, the trail switchbacks up onto the east wall of the canyon, then soon descends to Manzana Narrows Camp. Wedged in the narrow canyon, the oak- and willow-shaded camp offers pools for fishing and cooling-off.

Manzanita

40. Down Manzana Creek

HIGHLIGHTS: Manzana Creek is one of the delights of this part of Los Padres National Forest. Up-creek is Manzana Narrows, a narrow canyon where there are some fine pools for fishing and cooling off. Down-creek are some pleasant trail camps and a storied land that has attracted more than its share of eccentric settlers.

DISTANCE: Via Manzana Creek Trail to Potrero Canyon Camp, it's a 2½-mile round trip with a 100-foot elevation loss; to Coldwater Camp, 5 miles round trip with a 200-foot loss; to the Dabney Cabin, 14 miles round trip with a 500-foot elevation loss; to Manzana School House Camp, 17 miles round trip with a 700-foot loss.

TRANSPORTATION: From U.S. 101 in Santa Barbara, exit on California 154 and follow the latter highway over San Marcos Pass. Beyond Lake Cachuma, turn right on Armour Road and proceed 2½ miles to Happy Canyon Road. Make another right and continue 16 miles (Happy Canyon Road becomes Sunset Valley Road after passing an intersection at Figeroa Mountain Road). Just past the turnoff to Davy Brown Campground, the road crosses Davy Brown Creek; park just after the crossing.

MANZANA Creek forms the southern boundary of the San Rafael Wilderness, the first Wilderness Area in California set aside under the Federal Wilderness Act of 1964.

The lower stretch of the Manzana Creek Trail begins near a camp and creek named for William S. (Davy) Brown who kept a cabin here during his retirement years, 1879 to 1895.

The trail ends at the confluence of Manzana Creek and the Sisquoc River, where Hiram Preserved Wheat and his cult of religious fundamentalists from Kansas settled in. Wheat, it was said, had the power to heal with his hands. Hostile Indians were so impressed by the spiritual power of this white man that they inscribed his wagon with a sign indicating he was to be granted protection. Wheat and his followers stayed almost two decades, but a number of drought years and restrictions on homesteading, brought about by the creation of the Santa Barbara National Forest, combined to end the settlement.

As you hike Manzana Creek Trail, don't be surprised to come across stone foundations and chimneys, or perhaps an old bottle or bit of barbed wire, all that remains of a rough life in a rough land.

Manzana means "apple" in Spanish, and it's guessed that apple orchards once grew in the area. On second guess, it takes its name from *manzanita,* "little apple" in Spanish.

A mellow day hike would be a journey down-creek to Potrero Canyon Camp or Coldwater Camp. Intrepid hikers in good condition will enjoy the much longer treks to the Dabney Cabin or historic Manzana School House; this would be a lot of ground to cover in one day but there's little elevation loss or gain to slow you down. Use caution at the many creek crossings and expect to get your feet wet if the creek is high.

THE WALK: A San Rafael Wilderness sign marks the beginning of the Manzana Creek Trail. The path heads down-creek. Keep the creek on your right. A bit more than a mile's easy travel brings you to Potrero Canyon Camp in an oak woodland near the creek.

From the camp, you can push down-creek via either a high or low trail. The low trail crosses the creek many times as it winds to Coldwater Camp; the higher—and drier—high trail contours over digger pine- and chaparral-covered canyon walls. Coldwater Camp, set among pine and oak, is a fine place for a picnic. Even during dry years, water bubbles up from the creek bedrock, hence the camp's name.

Beyond the camp, the trail crosses Manzana Creek several more times before arriving at Dabney Cabin. The cabin, built by Charles Dabney in 1914, is leased by Santa Barbara's Sierra Club.

More creek crossings follow until you reach Manzana School House Camp, located near the confluence of Manzana Creek and the Sisquoc River. One-room Manzana School House, built at the turn of the century and now a County Historical Landmark, still stands.

Short Walks and Special Stops

Stevens Park

Pack a picnic and head for this delightful oak-shaded retreat at the outskirts of the city. Take the 1½-mile round-trip Jesusita Trail, a self-guided interpretive nature trail that meanders along with San Roque Creek. The path points out the special flora of the canyon—the coast live oaks and various creekside plants, as well as a Chumash Indian grinding rock, where acorns were pulverized into meal.

After the nature trail ends, Jesusita Trail continues 3½ more miles to Inspiration Point, then connects with Tunnel Road above Mission Canyon. (See Walk #30).

To reach Stevens Park, take the MTD bus along State Street to San Roque Road. Walk up San Roque to Calle Fresno, go left, then make a right on Canon Drive, and another quick right into Stevens Park.

If you're driving: From upper State Street turn north on San Roque Road. Turn left on Calle Fresno, then make an almost immediate right on Canon Drive, then another quick right into Stevens Park.

Tucker's Grove County Park

After the 1990 Painted Cave Fire blackened this park, the native chaparral and oak woodland recovered quickly. Today, the park closely resembles the attractive destination it was before the devastating blaze.

San Antonio Creek Trail begins at the upper end of the park's picnic area and follows San Antonio Creek 1¾ miles to the Highway 154 bridge. Oaks and grassy meadows are highlights of this quiet walk.

Take the MTD bus to Cathedral Oaks Road and Turnpike Road. Driving: From Highway 154, exit on Foothill Road/Cathedral Oaks Road and head west a mile to Tucker's Grove County Park. San Antonio Creek Trail begins at the upper picnic ground, called Kiwanis Meadow.

San Ysidro Creek Preserve

"When you walk through the preserve you have no idea you're in the middle of Montecito," declares Linda Krieger of the Land Trust for Santa Barbara County, the group that worked to secure 44 acres of oak woodland open space alongside San Ysidro Creek.

The Land Trust managed to secure 44 acres (homes were built on the other acreage) of a 120-acre estate once belonging to avid polo player Elmer Boeske. About two miles of trail loops through this brand-new preserve in the heart of residential Montecito. The paths explore an oak woodland, and pass rows of olive trees and eucalyptus. Because this is a preserve set aside for nature study and reflection rather than a park for picnicking and playing, this is a good place for a quiet walk.

To reach the San Ysidro Creek Preserve, exit Highway 101 on San Ysidro Road, head north briefly, and make a right on San Leandro Lane. Jog left on Hixon Road, then right again back onto San Leandro Lane, which you follow to a gate, pumphouse and preserve on the north side of the road.

Nojoqui Falls County Park

This park is a great rest stop or picnic spot for drives along Highway 101. *Nojoqui*, a Chumash word of unknown origin, was once the name of a rancheria under the jurisdiction of Mission La Purisima.

A quarter-mile long trail leads to the seasonal falls, located in pretty little grotto.

To reach the park, follow Highway 101 a few miles north of Gaviota Pass, exit on Alisal Road and continue 1½ miles to the park.

Information Sources

(ALL PREFIXES ARE 805)

Santa Barbara Conference & Visitors Bureau
510-A State Street, Santa Barbara, CA 93101
966-9222

Accomodations Santa Barbara
3344 State Street, Santa Barbara, CA 93105
687-9191

Hot Spots
36 State Street, Santa Barbara, CA 93101
564-1637

El Capitan/Refugio State Beaches
968-1033

El Presidio de Santa Barbara State Historic Park
123 E. Canon Perdido, Santa Barbara, CA 93101
966-9719

Los Padres National Forest
6144 Calle Real, Goleta, CA 93117
683-6711

Mission Santa Barbara
Los Olivos and Laguna Streets, Santa Barbara, CA 93101
682-4149

Nature Conservancy Visitor Center
213 Stearns Wharf, Santa Barbara, CA 93101
962-9111

Santa Barbara Botanic Garden
1212 Mission Canyon Road, Santa Barbara, CA 93105
682-4726

Santa Barbara County Courthouse
1100 Anacapa Street, Santa Barbara, CA 93101
962-6464

Santa Barbara County Parks
610 Mission Canyon Road, Santa Barbara, CA 93105
568-2461

Santa Barbara Historical Museum
136 East De la Guerra Street, Santa Barbara, CA 93101
966-1601

Santa Barbara Museum of Art
1130 State Street, Santa Barbara, CA 93101
963-4364

Santa Barbara Museum of Natural History
2559 Puesta del Sol Road, Santa Barbara, CA 93105
682-4334

Santa Barbara Parks and Recreation Department
620 Laguna Street, Santa Barbara, CA 93102
564-5418

Santa Barbara Zoological Gardens
500 Ninos Drive, Santa Barbara, CA 93103
962-6310

Sea Center
211 Stearns Wharf, Santa Barbara, CA 93101
962-0885

Stearns Wharf
Santa Barbara, CA 93101
564-5518

Annual Events

JANUARY

New Year's Day Hang Gliding Festival: *Precision flying contests off the ocean bluffs.*

Whale Watching (through March): *Boat tours in the Santa Barbara Channel for a look at migrating California gray whales.*

MARCH

Santa Barbara International Film Festival: *Two weeks of premieres and screenings of U.S. and foreign films.*

Santa Barbara International Orchid Show: *A horticultural happening.*

APRIL

Santa Barbara Arts Festival: *Two weeks of art exhibitions, music, theatre, dance.*

Santa Barbara County Vintner's Festival: *Celebrate the fruit of the vine in the Santa Ynez Valley.*

MAY

Cinco de Mayo Festival: *Celebration with mariachi music, folk dancing, food and fun.*

I Madonnari Italian Street Painting Festival: *Chalk paintings on the pavement of the Old Mission.*

JUNE

Santa Barbara County Fair: *Arts and crafts, rodeo and livestock show.*

Summer Solstice Parade: *Celebrate the longest day of the year with whimsical costumes, music and dance.*

Santa Barbara Writer's Conference: *Private workshops, public lectures.*

JULY
Semana Nautica: *Summer festival of land and water sports.*
Independence Day Parade and Concert
Santa Barbara Greek Festival: *Be Greek for a weekend with food, music and dancing.*

AUGUST
Old Spanish Days (Fiesta): *Five-day festival with parades, dances, concerts and costume parties celebrating Santa Barbara's heritage.*
Fête Francaise: *Santa Barbara's French Festival. Très magnifique!*

SEPTEMBER
Concours d'Elegance: *Antique car show features some of the finest automobiles in the world.*

OCTOBER
Festa Italiana: *Celebrate Italian heritage with food, music and fun.*

DECEMBER
Christmas Parade: *Costume parade with bands and floats.*
Yuletide Boat Parade: *Local sailors decorate their craft.*

Index